Praise for *By Cunning & Craft*:

"There is craft and there is cunning. There is the struggle to get published at all. But there is also the chance that you will do something extraordinary. Peter Selgin illustrates the tricks, both basic and sophisticated. But greatness is what he's really interested in. He thrusts the readers into the company of those who wrote magnificently. Salinger is quoted, Hemingway, Thomas Mann, E.M. Forster, John Gardner. 'This book is for serious writers of all levels,' he writes in the beginning, and he's talking about intentions. If you mean to shoot for the stars, then this book is for you."

> —Benjamin Cheever, author of *The Plagiarist, The Partisan* and *The Good Nanny*

"Peter Selgin has written an excellent guide—witty, lucid, well-written—for beginning writers of fiction. In fact, any writer can learn from it."

> —Vivian Gornick, author of *The Situation and the Story: The Art of Personal Narrative*

"Cunning and craft, indeed: Within these pages Peter Selgin quotes Chekhov to the effect that, 'The writer's task is not to solve the problem but to state the problem correctly.'" What I admire most about *By Cunning & Craft* is its rare and inspired modesty—an ultimately stylish resistance to pledging more than Selgin (really anyone) can deliver. May many learn from this book."

> —Robert Polito, author of *Savage Art: A Biography of Jim Thompson* and Director of the New School Graduate Creative Writing Program

"Along with great advice, Selgin is pure pleasure to read."
—Alexander Steele, Dean of Faculty, Gotham Writers' Workshop

"A wonderfully helpful, thorough, and honest book about writing. *By Cunning & Craft* is filled with good sense, good advice, and many excellent examples of good writing. A book to read and read again with profit by the beginning, the middle, and the writer of many years."
—Sheila Kohler, author of *Cracks*, *Crossways*, and *The Children of Pithiviers*

"*By Cunning & Craft* is a masterpiece of writing about writing. If, like Scheherazade, you had to spin out a story under threat of death, this is the how-to book to read. It's filled with thoughtful, nuanced advice from a teacher/writer who actually writes—and writes beautifully and with great humor. The list of rejected stories is worth the price of the whole book."
—Nora Gallagher, author of *Things Seen and Unseen*, *Practicing Resurrection*, and *Changing Light*

"While Selgin steers readers away from common mistakes, offers caveats for particularly daunting technical approaches, and articulates his view of what constitutes good fiction, he also encourages readers to follow their intuitions and safeguard their visions. ...One can, with enough diligence and time, learn a great deal about the craft of fiction, but reading *By Cunning & Craft* should accelerate the process."
—Laura van den Berg, *The Literary Review*

BY CUNNING & CRAFT

PRACTICAL WISDOM FOR FICTION WRITERS

by PETER SELGIN

A Nine Lives
Edition

SERVING HOUSE BOOKS

By Cunning & Craft:
Practical Wisdom for Fiction Writers

© 2007, 2012 by Peter Selgin

Originally published in hardcover by Writers Digest Books, an imprint of F+W Publications, Inc., Cincinnati, Ohio.

ISBN: 978-0-9858495-3-5
Cover illustration: Daniela Tordi
Serving House Books logo by Barry Lereng Wilmont

A Nine Lives Edition
Published by Serving House Books
Copenhagen, Denmark and Florham Park, NJ

www.servinghousebooks.com

First Serving House Books Edition 2012

BY CUNNING & CRAFT
PRACTICAL WISDOM FOR FICTION WRITERS

Contents:

INTRODUCTION:
The Case for Cunning & Craft

"All good writing is swimming underwater
and holding your breath."
—F. Scott Fitzgerald

INTRODUCTION:
THE CASE FOR CUNNING AND CRAFT

1. FICTION AND TRUTH

"Art is the lie that tells the truth."—Picasso

Someone once described a fiction writer as someone who, while still a child, told a lie and it felt good. But if fiction is a lie, it's a lie of a special order, a lie that tells the truth.

What do I mean? I mean that in his or her own way the fiction writer is as obsessed with precision as a thermonuclear technician, or a cardiac surgeon. The difference between a fiction writer and an ordinary liar is that the writer is someone who, while pulling your chain, feels compelled to get it just right, down to (for instance) the choice between a long dash and a comma to divide two parts of a sentence, or between 'powdery' and 'pale' as modifiers for a blue sky.

To the fiction writer such things matter. It matters that your protagonist's name is Henry and not Hank, and that he wears suspenders and not a belt, and that those suspenders have grown frayed from Hank's habit of hooking his thumbs under them. All such small details matter, because they form the substance of what John Gardner, in *The Art of Fiction,* calls a "continuous fictional dream." In writing fiction you weave dreams for your reader, and where either language or content falters the fabric is rent and readers slip through. Result: disappointment, dismay, or worse, readers cursing you for destroying the world they had so happily inhabited.

When, at a fictional cocktail party, Lilith chooses an hors d'oeuvre from the tray, she'd better make the right choice (devilled egg or pig-in-a-blanket?). The smallest false move can set off a chain-reaction of inauthentic character responses, undermining the fragile authenticity of a fictional world. At some devoutly-wished-for point in our writing, our characters turn into real people, and when we fail to respond authentically even to their most trivial wishes and urges we kill them off as living willful beings and turn them into puppets, and the fictional worlds they inhabit collapse.

That's what I mean by the fictional truth.

Making the right conscious choices sometimes works. The rest of the time we need to appeal to our instincts. Keats wrote, "I am certain of nothing but the holiness of the heart's affections and the truth of imagination." And the truth of imagination doesn't live in our brains: it inhabits some lower organ, the seat of our instincts.

2. What This Book Hopes to Teach

This is a book for serious fiction writers of all levels—from beginner to advanced and beyond, including accomplished authors wishing to fine-tune their craft. It aims to provide actionable advice, and plenty of it, yet offers no glib formulas or panaceas. Those seeking a writing guide that tells them, in so many words, that writing fiction is easy and that anyone can do it, should probably look elsewhere. Such guides exist and are hugely popular. As is so often the case, the truths of the matter are less obviously appealing, and are as follows: that writing fiction is indeed hard, that it takes time and energy and effort, that if everyone could do it it wouldn't be worth doing; at any rate, it would be no more worth doing than riding a bicycle, or whistling.

The bright side of this bad news being that anyone who wants to badly enough can learn, and learn well, and that all that's really needed, by way of talent, is determination. (You'll notice I didn't say "sheer determination." That would have been a cliché).

And so, assuming that you're determined and that, at least as far as writing is concerned, you're willing to take yourself as seriously as I'm willing to take you (and I intend to take you *very* seriously), then this book has something to teach you.

But if writing is an instinctive process, how can this or any book teach you how to write?

Part of the answer is that instinct alone isn't enough. To produce a work of art, technique must also be brought to bear. When instinct and technique merge seamlessly, I call the result *cunning*.

Cunning: "skillful ingenuity in doing something."

That said, I'm not going to teach you how to write. That is, I'm not going to teach you how to put words on paper; you already know how to do that. I'll give you pointers for writing first drafts, and talk about where ideas and inspirations come from, and suggest ways to guard against the intimidations and indignities of the dreaded White Page. Mostly, though, I'm going to teach you how to look at what you've already written, to see it for what it really is, and—if it isn't already publishable—help you make it so.

Publishable, that's the standard we'll be aiming for: what a sophisticated and discerning reader, i.e., an editor at a quality literary review or journal, or at a commercial publishing house, might conceivably pass along to her peers for further consideration.

How to apply technique to instinct and merge them into cunning: that's what I'm going to teach you. Whatever else they may say to the contrary, that's what all good fiction writing books and classes are really about. Though exercises and mantras may help get you started, no one can tell you how, exactly, to get that first rush of ideas on paper; that's between you and your private muse. Inspiration may find you in a dream, or in a public restroom. It may strike you like a bolt of lightning as you stroll the Boulevard du Montparnasse on a sunny day, or creep up on you slowly, like mildew on a shower curtain. You may write your first drafts sunk deep into leather in your book-lined study, or on a hilltop in Tennessee, or (as John Cheever did, supposedly) in your BVDs in a Manhattan apartment building's basement. Or follow Victor Hugo's lead and, standing naked on a rooftop in your house in the Channel Islands, pour a bucket of ice water over your head before entering the glass cage you call your "lookout" and writing for hours standing at a lectern. However you write it, that first draft is no one's business, really, but your own.

My business is to help you come up with ideas to write from, and to show you, once you have written something, where to go from there.

3. WHY I WRITE, AND WHY I TEACH

When I was an art student at Pratt Institute, in studio painting class, my professor stepped up behind me and stood watching me work. After a few beats he said, loud enough for everyone else in the class to hear, "Know what you are, Selgin? You're an artistic illiterate."

My first impulse was to strangle the man. But later, as I walked back to my dorm, something in me began to suspect that my painting professor was right. I drew well; I had no trouble mixing colors. I worked quickly and easily, and the results were superficially pleasing. And this was my problem. My paintings were glib; they were shallow. They skated along surfaces of shape, colors, and lines and never dove under. I wanted to go deeper, but my facility prevented me.

That same evening, I was watching the small, portable black and white TV in my dorm room when suddenly Richard Burton's face filled the screen. I kept watching, mesmerized, until I realized I was watching Mike Nichol's film version of the play *Who's Afraid of Virginia Woolf?* by Edward Albee. The next morning I went to the Pratt library where, among the glass-floored stacks, I found a copy of the play. I sat down right there on the glass floor and read it, amazed to find what had gripped me the evening before reduced to a series of black marks on paper, to printed words and sentences that—through Richard Burton's cherubic lips and sonorous Welsh baritone—had carried me off to another world. I'd never realized before that words could be so moving, that they could penetrate so deeply. By the time I turned the last page of Albee's play I'd made up my mind. To hell with painting: I'd be a writer; I'd write.

At first I wrote plays, lousy ones, each with a "mesmerizing" speech at its center, along with long letters to indulgent friends. After a while I tried my hand at stories and even a novel. Meanwhile, since I hadn't been all that much of a reader before, I made up for lost time by reading everything I could. Over the next ten or so years my writing got better, and eventually I published.

I taught myself the hard way, through trial and error, at the expense of readers' patience and forests of trees.

And this is why I teach: because I don't think you need to sacrifice ten years and an ecosystem to learn to write fiction. Nor is it necessary for you to commit every possible literary sin in order to profit from it. This book aims to save you time and to save our forests.

4. How to Use this Book

Writing a story or a novel isn't like building a ship or like baking a cake. There are no blueprints or recipes to follow, no glib step-by-step formulas. If there are, at best they'll produce the verbal equivalent of cake from a box or a painting by numbers.

Therefore, though I've arranged these lessons with the hope of having them build off each other, their order in this book is otherwise arbitrary. You don't start with characters and add plot, or vice-versa, or begin with a scene, stir in a pound of dialogue, then add a dollop of description and a pinch of poetry. Fictional works—novels especially—tend to be written two ways: all at once or in bits and pieces, with the author holding a large, overall concept in his head while at the same time collecting—as a beachcomber collects rocks, shells and starfish from the shore—small yet significant details. Look into almost any fiction writer's notebook and you'll see the equivalent of a compost heap of words: working titles, scene fragments, character biographies, historical, scientific and technical trivia on arcane subjects like mercury poisoning or the Indigo Wars. In a word: chaos. Out of this chaos of ideas and information, by applying "cunning" as defined and conveyed by the lessons in this book, you fashion the ordered world of a story or novel.

And though there's no strict order in which those lessons should be learned or applied, I suggest that you first read them through in order. Then, as particular issues arise in your creative work, refer to them ad hoc with a greater sense of context.

5. SOME NOTES ON FIRST DRAFTS

"All first drafts are excrement."—Hemingway

Though first drafts are your business, still, I can give you some advice about them.

When writing your first drafts, don't edit. A writer friend of mine who owns a collection of hats wears one, a scarlet baseball cap with "Kerouac" stitched in gold on the visor, while writing her first drafts, and another—Chinese, tutti-frutti, shaped like a funnel—when revising them. This may be going too far (I also think it odd that the funnel should serve for the editor). Still, it makes a good point: Though they share the goal of creating a literary work, editing and writing are different disciplines requiring different temperaments, different skills. We draft instinctively, with our emotions; we revise consciously, with our intellects. We dive into those feelings, hold our breath, and swim underwater.

Not usually one to mince words, Hemingway minced one when he called all first drafts excrement. We know what Hem *really* meant. He meant that we shouldn't give a damn what we get on paper as long as we get *something* on paper. He went on to say, "The only thing a first draft needs to do is get written." I agree. Then (he might have added) it needs to get rewritten, again and again, until every sentence rings like a bell.

We'll get to that.

When it comes to first drafts, Voltaire said "the perfect is the enemy of the good." In our eagerness to produce pristine first drafts we may produce nothing at all. Rather than work with grim determination as our taskmaster, hunched over, knitting our foreheads and gritting our teeth at our desks, why not see first drafts as an opportunity for play?

Here is a piece of advice given far too infrequently to fiction authors (who on the whole tend to take themselves too seriously): *Have more fun.* "The secret of genius," wrote Thomas Henry Huxley, "is to carry the spirit of childhood into maturity." Be a genius, I say, and carry that spirit into writing your first draft.

Don't chisel perfect sentences into stone, or try to. That's no way to write a first draft. Don't even think that you're writing; think that you're dancing, or conducting a symphony, or chasing moonbeams, or soaping windows. Don't be a slave to grammar or syntax, or even to meaning. Write to the sound of words, not to their logic—not at first. Be guided by rhythms, hues, textures, game theory, Astrological charts, whim. Be bold, be devilish; be outrageous. Forget about readers; tickle *yourself*. Should doubts, misgivings or disgust arise during this honeymoon, shoo, shoo them away. If they persist, consider the possibility that bride and groom (artist and subject) aren't truly meant for each other. However you manage it, try, at this juncture, to have at least *some* fun.

Roll through that first draft like thunder. This is what Jack Kerouac did infamously and to an extreme when he banged out a draft of *On the Road* in a three-week marathon on a continuous, 120-foot long scroll of teletype paper (so he wouldn't have to pause between sheets).

Must you write first drafts this way? No. John Updike and William Styron are two authors on record as favoring a more measured approach, settling down to the task of writing only after having plotted their works fully in their heads, cutting each jewel of a sentence to perfection before moving on to the next, working as slowly as glaciers. Some writers literally don't let themselves proceed unless every word that has gone before is perfect. That's *their* neurosis. And all writers have their neuroses, whether it's sharpening a jar full of round pencils before each day's work (the hexagonal ones irritated John Steinbeck's writer's callous), or reading a passage from the Bible (as Willa Cather used to do), not out of piety, but for the rhythms of its prose. Capote wrote in bed; Thomas Wolfe used the top of a refrigerator for a desk. You may choose to dress in full armor and listen to Gregorian chants: whatever gets the ideas on paper.

Letting the words pour out, that's the less obsessive approach. "Verbal finger painting," a writer friend of mine calls it. Slap down thoughts in thick sloppy strokes; use a fat brush and low-grade house latex; throw some paint onto that glaringly white page, see if the broad strokes don't add up to a story, or start to.

When I was a child my father and I would play a game. I'd draw five lines on a piece of paper, a line being a squiggle, a circle, a jagged scrawl—anything I could draw without lifting pencil off paper. Then I'd say to my papa, "Draw me a picture," and, incorporating those five lines, he'd draw something for me.[1]

Those five lines, that was a rough draft.

There's no one right way to get words on paper. Whatever your process, you want to find a way to get at your instincts, to access the part of yourself that knows more about life than you and your brain.

At this first draft stage, writing fiction is a form of creative subjugation. It's submitting yourself to the deeper, wiser authority of imagination, appealing to the holiness of the heart, with every word a prayer, and every sentence a leap of faith.

---

1 A telephone, usually.

6. Loving Words & Reading as Writers

So far I've mentioned two essentials that fiction writers should bring to their process: a love of imaginative (as distinct from literal) truth, and a prayerful willingness to suspend logical judgment and allow the imaginative truths in us to reach the page. This willingness includes the willingness to be imperfect and, hence, to (possibly) fail.

To convey those inner truths you need some tools, namely computer, printer, words, grammar, and punctuation. All of these tools, down to the smallest comma, should have your love and respect. Words especially. To a writer, words are as solid as stones: some hefty, others like pebbles; some bright, others dull. We hold them in our hands and feel their weight; we hurl them out into the world knowing they may cause injury to others, or bounce back and hit us square in the face. We care deeply about words. We fear and love them. We care about words and we care about truth, and try to get at the latter by means of the former.

You need one more thing. You need to love literature, to love reading, and you must read: widely, ravenously, promiscuously, with a greedy lust for others' words.

> *"Don't ask me who has influenced me. A lion is made up of the lambs he has digested, and I've been reading all my life."*
> —George Seferis

You want to read the best that's out there, and some of the worst, too. Read with pleasure, but also with a technician's eye on how things are done. How does she slip into that flashback? How does she slip out? See how he punctuates that dialogue, the spontaneous dash, the cerebral semicolon? Why that paragraph break there? Why this white space here? Notice how easily that metaphor is extended, how effortless and inevitable it seems.

People who don't love to read don't make great writers. That should be obvious but isn't, not in this age where most of our fictional dreams come to us not via words on paper, but through images and sounds from a movie, television, or computer screens, in a form that does nearly all the imagining for us. And though movies can be wonderful, you can't learn to write fiction from them.

But you can learn from books. Not to put myself out of a perfectly pleasant job, but the greatest writing teachers in the world are the novels and short story collections on your shelves. With such great instructors, why aren't we all masters of our craft? Because though we read, we don't read as *writers*, with an eye on technique. From here on, if you aren't already doing so, you'll want to read as a writer.

7. Cunning & Craft

> *"A writer is someone for whom writing is more difficult than it is for other people."*
> —Thomas Mann

A first draft isn't an end, but a beginning. The job begun by inspiration, intuition, and instinct, must be completed consciously, by cunning and through craft. At some point we need to know what we're doing. Having written:

An entire platoon ducked from grave to grave in
the Capuchin Cemetery high on the hill overlook-
ing the town. The entire platoon was scared.
—John Hersey, *A Bell for Adano*

it's useful to know that you're writing from an omniscient
viewpoint, past tense, that you have entered into the consciousness not just of a single man, but of an entire platoon.
It helps to know because only by knowing can you communicate your intentions—not only to others in a writing class
or workshop, but to yourself. (Assuming that you meant to
do what you have in fact done. Maybe you did, and maybe
you didn't.)

Supposing you wrote:

All this happened while I was walking around
starving in Christiania—that strange city no one
escapes from until it has left its mark on him.
—Knut Hamsun, *Hunger*

Now you're writing a first person narrative, a frank con-
fessional painted in the grainy sepia tones of memory, but
also tinged with magic. Why know this? If our instincts are
guiding us perfectly, then arguably we don't need to know.
But if (as is often the case) they aren't, and things aren't going so well, then we need to ask questions, and those questions can be clearly formed only through a correct understanding of the mechanics of fictional prose.

Example: If you've written a story about a woman supposedly afflicted with Alzheimer's, whose actions are de-

mented, in what's called a close (limited to her viewpoint) third person point of view in language not only vivid and rich, but that conveys a comprehensive understanding of the world, then either you must suspect the medical diagnosis, or question the narrative technique. In such an instance your instincts have most likely failed you.

Or say you tell the story of a victim from the victim's point of view, with the intention of skewering the assailant. But the strategy backfires, because what was supposed to be a narrative feels more like a diatribe or an assault—and not against the victim, but against all parents who spank their children, or whatever. That you, the author, feel sympathy (or lack thereof) toward a character may not be the best reason for telling his story; in fact, it may be the worst reason. We write to understand, and read for the same reason. That we find it impossible to sympathize with a character may be a good reason to see things from their perspective, or to try.

On the other hand we can't afford to love or sympathize with our characters blindly, either. We have to see them clearly, and even coldly. But we are not machines, and sooner or later even our best instincts run us into walls.

Here's Toni Morrison running on sheer beginner's gall:

> Here is the house. It is green and white. It has
> a red door. It is very pretty. Here is the family.
> Mother, Father, Dick and Jane live in the green-
> and-white house. They are very happy. See Jane.
> She has a red dress.

When she wrote *The Bluest Eye*, her first novel, Morrison was savvy enough (she worked in publishing) to dare to dip us into her fictional world using the style of a grade school reading primer, knowing—or anyway hoping—that she'd get away with it. She did. But she also knew that such a tactic has a short shelf life, that more than a page or two of this and most readers would bail. Indeed, on page 3 she switches from Dick-and-Jane omniscient to a straight first-person past-tense "prologue," and from there into a straightforward, present-tense first-person narrative that dominates the rest of the novel.

Confused by all of these terms? Don't worry, we'll get to them, by and by.

First, though, you need to get into some good habits.

8. Habits

"I love being a writer. What I can't stand is the paperwork."
—Peter DeVries

What do writers wish for almost as much as they wish for talent, fortune and fame? Discipline. The word itself is enough to strike terror in some of us. Unless it comes in pill or powder form no one can give you discipline. But teachers can give you deadlines and exercises, and I can suggest some good habits to get into.

Keep a journal. Carry a notebook with you at all times and in which you record random observations, ideas, sentences, titles, and so on. You may start stories here, or end them. Though you may record your daily experiences, a journal needn't be as dogmatically routine as a diary. It should mainly be a place to daydream, to free-associate, to splash around in the mud puddle of language.

[23]

Write every day. Even if only a letter to the local newspaper, or to a friend, try to keep your hand in. "Nulla dies sine linea," or not a day without a line, as the painter Appelles said. Want a number? Okay, how about five hundred words a day? That's two pages, two pages of *anything*.

Put your ego in the closet. Egos can't write. Well, they can, but they tend to write poorly. In its single-minded quest for praise the ego strains for effect, it sacrifices clarity and sincerity for cleverness and complexity. When you find yourself showing off, that's your ego writing. Grab the keyboard away, the quicker the better, before you let yourself be seduced by its desperate charms. Half the time, it's not you reaching for the online Thesaurus, but your ego. Tell it to write its own stuff and leave yours alone.

Wish not to be a writer, but to write. A writer, after all, is someone who writes. And too often the wish to be a writer is at odds with the impulse to write (or its lack). "Apply the seat of the pants to the seat of the chair," was Clare Booth Luce's great advice to writers. Which is another way of saying "love the 'paperwork.'" Myself, when asked if I'm a writer, I answer, "When I'm writing, yes."

Be clear. This can mean "write simply," but doesn't have to. Whatever aesthetic or methods you follow or apply, your prime motive should be to communicate effectively and clearly. Or, as Joseph Conrad describes his task to his readers, "by the power of the written word, to make you hear, to make you feel—above all to make you see. That and no more."

9. RULES

One more rule that supersedes all:

THERE ARE NO RULES

For an artist, it's better to risk catastrophe than to fail by playing it safe. If somewhere in the pages that follow I advise against use of the omniscient in short stories, or urge you never to state what's implied, or declare that specific trumps general and concrete beats abstract, or warn you to beware of adverbs and to shun Latinisms—remember that these and all rules are made to be broken by you at your own risk. And artists—as opposed to journeymen and hacks—should take risks: calculated ones based on experience and knowledge. My telling you to forget forever phrases like *at that point in time* or *proceeded to* or *the vast majority* is no reason for you to do so; nor should you, out of respect for me or anyone else, favor *bought* over *purchased*. Should your superior instincts compel you to do so, you should feel more than free at any time to ignore and/or sneer at pedagogues like me, and thumb your nose at any or all conventions and opinions. Stick to your artistic and grammatical guns. You want your character to *purchase* a bottle of whisky? Fine. Go ahead; knock yourself out. Make my day.

My only hope is that you leave these pages with a better understanding of yourself as a writer than when you entered them, that you begin to hear the sound of your own voice, and that your words hone closer to your intentions than they would have when you started.

One last tale before I end this introduction. A former student of mine, Elliot, has been my biggest success story. Already in his fifties when he first came to me, the man could not put three words together without committing a cliché. Where his prose wasn't rife with clichés it was melodramatic and sentimental in the extreme.

That was a few years ago. Since then Elliot has worked hard at his writing and has also read a great deal. He has evicted his ego, applied the seat of his pants to the seat of his chair, dredged truth from the depths of imagination and memory, and conveyed those truths clearly through carefully weighed words. Sentiment has turned into toughness; clichés to poetry:

> We started off at Harper's Marina, a rusted metal building surrounded by a chain link fence off a gravel road near Rte. 70. A sign on the fence read "Harper's Marina—Serving Barnegat Bay, New Jersey Since 1953" in block letters above a sun-faded picture of smiling purple crabs crawling next to open clam shells at the bottom of blue water. The sign felt friendly and I liked the idea that the marina and I were the same age.

These days Elliot publishes regularly. Just the other day he sent me a new story of his to read.

I wish I'd written it.

CHAPTER I:
PEOPLE

*"Begin with an individual, and before you know it you find
that you have created a type; begin with a type, and you find
that you have created—nothing."*
—F. Scott Fitzgerald, *"The Rich Boy"*

I. PEOPLE

1. FICTION IS ABOUT PEOPLE

On the oak-paneled wall of his den, my father-in-law keeps a varnished wooden plaque. The plaque reminds him that, "Great minds talk about ideas, average minds talk about things, and small minds talk about people." An injunction against gossip.

In fiction writing the hierarchy is reversed. What readers of fiction most want to learn about is people. Not ideas, opinions or philosophy; not *The Communist Manifesto, Robert's Rules of Order, The Merck Manual* or lore about nuclear submarines. Novels and short stories fascinate us because, as someone put it to Flannery O'Connor, they show us "how some folks would do." That's what fiction does best, why it gets written and read. Call it an enlightened form of gossip.

People are not fiction's main subject, they are its only subject. Ahab, Don Quixote, Leopold Bloom, Holden Caufield, Scarlet O'Hara, Miss Jean Brodie, Hamlet ... We remember the characters in fiction like real people we've grown to love, fear or despise. They fascinate us.

*"Since the novelist is himself a human being there is
an affinity between him and his subject matter which
is absent in any other forms of art."*—E. M. Forster

Some say, "I don't read fiction. When I read I want to
learn something; I don't want to waste time on stuff that's
not true." They are misguided. You can learn plenty from
other kinds of books. But if you want to learn about human nature, fiction's the place to go. Biographies, autobiog-
raphies and memoirs will take you only so deeply into the
human psyche. And what a politician or celebrity *says* about
himself and what he really thinks and feels are doubtlessly
different things. How else but through fiction can you stand
in a motel room with two adulterous lovers after a postcoital
quarrel, and see not only their gestures and the looks on their
faces, but what's in their heads? How else can you learn what
it's like to hack your landlady to death, or feel the "wham" of
a dose of heroin, or cower in a muddy trench in the Battle of
the Somme—and not just be told about it, but experience it
personally, viscerally?

Journalists misquote; nonfiction lies. Want the truth? Ask
a fiction writer. *I am certain of nothing but the holiness of the
heart's affections and the truth of imagination.* And the truth
of imagination doesn't lie. It doesn't lie because it taps into
the universal unconscious, the place where dreams and myths
shared by all of us are born. It is no less reliable a source of
truth than the deep instincts that prompt us to love and fear.

Fiction is our way into experiences that we'll never have,
into people we'll never know or meet—or want to, necessarily. Malcolm Lowry's drunken Consul *(Under the Volca-*

no) as a houseguest? No thank you. Between cloth or paper covers, though, I'll gladly have him over to dinner. I'll even take him to bed with me.

2. MOTIVATION

In *A Streetcar Named Desire*, Tennessee William's frazzled heroine, Blanche DuBois, calls death "the opposite of desire." To the extent that people want something they exist. This is especially true of fictional characters. Begin with a character who wants something, and you're off to a good start. On the other hand, those who want nothing from life exist as shadows, or like sticks of furniture in a bare room. From such people it's hard to extract a single solid action, let alone a whole plot.

> *"No fiction can have real interest if the central character is not an agent struggling for his or her own goals but a victim, subject to the whim of others."*
> —John Gardner

People who read fiction aren't interested in shadows or furniture, they're interested in people, in characters. What drives them, what do they want, why do they want it? And how do they go about getting (or not getting, or losing) it?

The answer to such questions is a novel or a story.

There are exceptions. Think of Ralph Ellison's *Invisible Man*, or Jacob Horner in John Barth's *The End of the Road*—a character so paralyzed with indecision he can't get up from a bus terminal bench. We tend to think of such passive characters as ciphers, blank outlines waiting to be filled in. Yes, effective and even great stories have been written about characters with so little willpower that the winds of fate blow them hither and yon with little resistance. Such stories we call "existential" (Abert Camus' *The Stranger*, Sartre's *Nausea;* Walker Percy's *The Moviegoer)*. In them the anti-hero's decision to do nothing amounts to a philosophy or stance: an antidecision. But then you must know that this is your theme, and know how hard it is to pull off.

Motivation is contingent with desire, and—like everything else in fiction—most vividly conveyed through action. If a character's desires are vague and abstract, the first part of your job will be to render them concrete and specific. Witness (and I use the word purposefully, since in dramatizing your material you turn readers into witnesses) the following example of motivation revealed through action:

> He took out a pile of shirts and began throwing them, one by one, before us, shirts of sheer linen and thick silk and fine flannel, which lost their folds as they fell and covered the table in many-colored disarray. While we admired he brought more and the soft rich heap mounted higher—shirts with stripes and scrolls and plaids in coral and apple-green and lavender and faint orange, with monograms of Indian blue. Suddenly, with a strained sound, Daisy bent her head into the shirts and began to cry stormily.
>
> "They're such beautiful shirts," she sobbed, her voice muffled in the thick folds. "It makes me

sad because I've never seen such—such beautiful shirts before."
—F. Scott Fitzgerald, *The Great Gatsby*

On a purely abstract level, Gatsby wishes to impress Daisy and thus win her affection. More concretely, he does so by becoming fabulously wealthy by whatever means are possible—namely, by aligning himself with certain underworld elements. But we are still dealing with abstractions. Dramatically, specifically, what does Jay Gatsby *do* with his dubiously achieved wealth in order to achieve his goal? For one thing, he buys a plethora of silk shirts and waves them—like flags—in front of Daisy's susceptible eyes.

As a fiction writer your task isn't to tell us what characters want and therefore who they are, but to show us how far they are willing to go to get it, and by what means.

3. BUILDING CHARACTERS

To write about people effectively we need to know who they are. You can't feel sympathy for someone you don't know. That doesn't mean you have to love or even to like a character. You need only be interested, curious. Having already made up your mind that the man living alone in a fishing shack by the river—the one who walks with a limp and wears green coveralls—is evil, why write about him? Writing is, after all, an act of exploration through which we learn answers to questions raised by our raw material, our characters, and their situations. If you already feel you know the answers, why bother writing?

When writing about someone, it's not a bad thing to start with a question you'd like answered. Why, for instance, does an educated, cultured, and worldly man kidnap a pubescent girl and drive her across America, from motel room to motel room? In answer to that question Nabokov gives us *Lolita*. Why does a man live underground amid 1,369 light bulbs? To find out, read *Invisible Man*. Why does the captain of a whaling ship risk life and limb, his own and his crew's, in pursuit of a white whale? Answer: *Moby-Dick*, or *The Whale*.

To answer the questions raised by our characters and their desires it helps to know as much about them as possible, starting with basic, vital statistics. How old are they? Where were they born? Family background, level of education, employment and medical history, likes and dislikes: determining factors, all. How do we learn these things? By writing them down. When a character fails to live in your pages, try this: write a one-page biography summarizing their life history. No need for poetry, just the facts.

Where do these facts come from? From the imagination, which doesn't lie. Through the sublime power of the declarative sentence, the moment we state them in writing the fruits of our imaginative instincts transform themselves into facts.

In one class of mine, a student wrote an imaginary biography of a woman, Sally Schmidt, who had been a Navy scuba diver in Vietnam. Were there Navy scuba divers in Vietnam, let alone female Navy scuba divers? The author had no idea. Yet none of the fourteen other students in the class questioned the authority of this bold and specific claim. Later, we learned that there had indeed been women Navy divers in Vietnam. Chalk one up for the truth of imagination.

As you dredge up these facts from your imagination, you will learn Sally's background. And knowing that background, you will know how she responds when a strange man pinches her in a Neapolitan bus station (given that she was a Navy diver in Vietnam, I doubt she'd take it kindly).

Your reader doesn't need to know all this background; you do. In fact it's better if you don't tell too much about your characters, just what the reader needs to know to get the most out of your plot. Don't paint every leaf on the tree. The same applies to physical descriptions. A few telling details: Jasper combs his hair like Hitler and likes to spit between the gap in his front teeth. The rest the reader will supply with his or her imagination, which writes better than you or I or any of us can.

In your notebooks, record subtle nuances of character based upon observation: how people dress, their gestures and voices, the things they say and do. Notice how your father-in-law cups his fingers around a stingy dollar bill to hide it as he hands it to the parking valet? That young woman yammering on her cell phone at a cafe? Notice how she flips back her hair while talking (could she be talking to the guy she slept with last night?). Observe closely and carefully and you'll learn a lot about human nature. Pay special attention to those moments in life when stereotypes collapse, or are dismayingly upheld.

Note, too, the things people do when they feel they're not being noticed. Like the man who, walking ahead of you down the sidewalk in his spiffy suit, glances at every shop window he passes, intent not on the goods on display, but on his own spiffy reflection.

The expected ways in which people behave are as important to note as the unexpected ways. People *do* cross their arms defiantly, and scratch themselves where they have no itches. They look to the floor when embarrassed or shy, and to the sky in search of release. Ever seen someone smile with their eyes? Sure you have. Ever seen someone smile with their lips only, while their eyes remain sad and dead? You have, but maybe you haven't noticed.

4. TYPES VS. STEREOTYPES

Convincing characters function both as individuals and as types. This sounds like a contradiction, but it's not. When we first encounter people, we often encounter them as types: the stilted intellectual, the jock, the charmer, the vixen, the prude, the square, the tweedy professor. As we get to know them, we see that they don't fit quite so snugly into these labels; their personalities spill over into unexpected areas. The jock reads Alexander Pope; while playing poker with his friends the slob drinks champagne (he also breaks open a brand new pair of socks every day); the milquetoast holds a fifth degree black belt. Some of these category-defying combinations, like the Bashful Librarian (who, in act 3, takes off her catty glasses, lets her hair down, and morphs into Ava Gardner) are themselves stereotypes to be avoided.

And what, exactly, is a stereotype? Simply a character not born or created by its author, but appropriated, ready-made, from previous works. Even assuming that Marion the Librarian is a realistic character, still, we find her uninteresting, having encountered her so often before in cheesy novels, plays, stories and movies (see: *The Music Man, The Rainmaker, Superman, Rocky,* etc.). A stereotype is the human equivalent of a cliché: a creation once fresh and exciting but which, through overuse, has worn out its welcome.

Since you'll be running into the term throughout this book, now is as good a time as any to say a few words about clichés. Martin Amis calls all good writing a war against cliché. "Not just the clichés of the pen," he writes, "but clichés of the mind and clichés of the heart." Clichés are ideas, scenarios, or strings of words—or any combination thereof—that, instead of being arrived at honestly by an author, have been snatched from a communal artistic recycling heap. The advantage of clichés: They cost nothing in time and effort; the disadvantage: They're worth what they cost. At best readers skip over them as one skips over something unpleasant on a sidewalk; at worst they foul up whatever they touch. Some of the world's most flagrant clichés ("it's raining cats and dogs") were once poetry worthy of Homer or Shakespeare. Whoever coined that phrase had cause to be proud. But you didn't, and neither did I, and should either of us commit that particular string of words to paper except as dialogue in the mouth of a dull character, we should be mortified. We're writers, not junk peddlers: We owe our readers fresh words to describe the rain.

So, a stereotype is a character cliché. The bottom line being this: Write characters; don't recycle them. Follow Fitzgerald's excellent advice and begin with an individual, someone who may share the characteristics of persons you know or have known, or of people you've only heard or read about. In fact it's probably best *not* to base characters on people you know too well, since this not only limits your imagination, but clutters it with specifics that may or may not serve your fictional character and the story you want to tell about or through them (it may also lead to embarrassing, hurtful, and potentially libelous situations).

Remember this, too: that though for sure we want our characters to be "real," they should be real not because they stand for living people in the actual world, but in their own, fictional terms. Fictional characters are made not of flesh and bones and blood but of *words.* Not words that signify something out there, in what we call reality, but that create their own reality on the page. The difference between the writer who tries to copy the world using words, and the writer who *makes* a world *out of* words, is the difference between tracing a picture and painting one.

5. ROUND VS. FLAT CHARACTERS

Characters who don't grow or change or surprise us in any way we call *flat* characters. The term, coined by E.M. Forster in *Aspects of the Novel,* sounds derogatory, but isn't meant to be. There is nothing wrong with flat characters. They may be types, but they aren't *stereotypes.*

For a good example of a flat character look at the detective in Graham Greene's *The End of the Affair.* This private eye (hired to spy on the woman with whom the protagonist has had an adulterous affair, to learn if she's now having an affair with someone else) is accompanied by his thirteen-year-old son, a snoop-in-training who seems far more competent than his dad. In a novel otherwise shot through with despair, you can see the possibilities for comic relief. Each time we encounter this unlikely duo we're amused and gratified, despite or perhaps because we know pretty much what to expect from them, since they are predictable, flat, characters.

Other examples of flat characters: the greedy landowners in John Steinbeck's *The Grapes of Wrath,* Nurse Ratched in Ken Kesey's *One Flew Over the Cuckoo's Nest.* In Harper Lee's *To Kill a Mockingbird,* Scout Finch's friend Dill (based, allegedly, on Lee's childhood friend, Truman Capote). Nearly all secondary characters in Dickens.

The key to creating flat characters without succumbing to stereotype is, again, to begin with specific, individual qualities rather than thinking in terms of types. Think of three teenage boys. One reads a lot, one often gets into trouble, the third is athletic and gregarious. Note how quickly—like an invading army—the stereotyping process seizes the imagination, supplying the "bookworm" with "Coke-bottle thick" glasses, the "juvenile delinquent" with a black leather jacket and a drunk/jailbird father, the "jock" with sandy blond hair and the Homecoming Queen as his main squeeze. Though scientists now claim it as the source of melatonin, I suspect that the mysterious pineal body, lodged deep in our brains, is in fact the source of stereotypes, hence they come so easily to us. To avoid them requires nothing more than vigilance: the ability to recognize and, once recognized, to subvert them. Give the jock the thick glasses (who says all jocks have 20-20 vision?). Let the bookworm toss a cherry bomb into the lavatory toilet (on which he has spent the last hour finishing Robert Musil's *The Man Without Qualities*). Make the delinquent's dad a Nobel Laureate and Mensa member. Do what you must, but smash those damned clichés. Then even your flat characters will charm and amuse us.

But flat characters serve a greater purpose than to charm or amuse. They often provide the static status quo against which we measure changes undergone by characters *not* flat, but round. Unlike flat characters, who fill minor or supporting roles, round characters play major or leading parts. They are multi-dimensional, complex, and subject to change, making them unpredictable and interesting. Flat characters may come in handy, but you don't want to read whole novels about them.

Some round characters: Huckleberry Finn, Colette's Chéri, Holden Caulfield, Blanche DuBois, Atticus Finch, Francis Phelan (the protagonist of William Kennedy's Pulizer Prize-winning novel about Albany bums, *Ironweed*) ... I could go on forever, since the main characters of all great or even good stories and novels are round.

6. WAYS OF EVOKING CHARACTER

Assuming that we know them well, how do we get our characters onto the page? How do we evoke them? One way is **through summary or physical description:**

> Robert Cohn was once middleweight boxing
> champion of Princeton. Do not think that I am

very much impressed by that as a boxing title, but it meant a lot to Cohn. He cared nothing for boxing, in fact he disliked it, but he learned it painfully and thoroughly to counteract the feeling of inferiority and shyness he had felt on being treated as a Jew at Princeton. ...
—Ernest Hemingway, *The Sun Also Rises*

[H]e sighed in relief in seeing her so like herself, her mouth barely touched with lipstick, her lower lip broad and often chapped, her upper lip short and drawn up by the nose—that little nose that was slightly flat, slightly crushed, ugly, Cambodian and inimitable—and those eyes especially, elongated like leaves, with their mingled green and gray, pale in the evening lamplight, darker in the morning.
—Colette, *Duo*

These descriptions tell rather than show; they are not dramatic, but expedient, the main advantage of summary being that it (usually) takes less space. In just a few pages we learn all about Robert Cohn's past—that is, we learn everything we need to know to appreciate what's coming, namely a dramatized scene. To have fleshed out Cohn's years at Princeton *dramatically* would have taken many more pages, if not a whole novel.

Colette's summary description, on the other hand, has to do mainly with her character's physical appearance. It can be argued that from it we learn more about the perceiver than about the object perceived, since beauty exists (so we're told) in the eyes of the beholder. Unless seen through the eyes of another character, as here, such descriptions of a character's looks tend to be static and to feel perfunctory. Later I'll discuss ways of making such inert descriptions active. For now, I simply want to acquaint you to the possibility of introducing information about characters through summary.

Before I go on to discuss more dramatic methods of evoking character, here's an example of character evoked not through action or through pure summary but through **summarized action:**

> This man who farts and belches and snores as well as laughs and kisses and holds her. Somehow this husband whose whiskers she finds each morning in the sink, whose shoes she must air each evening on the porch, this husband who cuts his fingernails in public, laughs loudly, curses like a man, and demands each course of dinner be served on a separate plate like at his mother's, as soon as he gets home, on time or late, and who doesn't care at all for music or telenovelas or romance or roses or the moon floating pearly over the arroyo, or through the bedroom window for that matter. ...
> —Sandra Cisneros, "Woman Hollering Creek"

From the earlier example of Gatsby flinging his silk shirts in "many-colored disarray," we could assign certain characteristics to the title character. We could say that he is *wealthy, materialistic, naive, a show-off, childish, desperate, pathetic,* and so on. Those are the abstract terms (opinions) that Fitzgerald, through cunning dramatization, avoids.

Similarly, in the above excerpt, Cisneros doesn't tell us that the husband in question is crude, demanding, selfish, unromantic, or a slob. Here, too, we are shown his behavior, not through a single, fleshed-out scene, but through a summary of his actions. Either way, actions speak louder and more effectively than mere words, among other reasons because they let readers draw their own conclusions based on *evidence,* painting a far more vivid, visceral and convincing picture than can be achieved by hurling every adjective in the dictionary.

How to give more *telling actions* to your characters? Here, too, the key is motivation. Again, ask yourself, *What does the character want?* and then, *How far is she willing to go to get it?* If the answer to the second question is *Not very far,* at least you know why you're having trouble writing active scenes, because a character who doesn't want anything, or doesn't want it badly enough, is not going to act. Give her the necessary motivation, situate her such that she doesn't simply want the thing in question, but *needs* it in order to survive physically or emotionally, and your character will do things that show us, vividly, who she is.

Add **dialogue** to the mix, and the portrait grows more vivid still:

> … the stranger opened the door [of the cafe] with a determined thrust of his arm. He passed between the tables with a rapid, springy step, and stopped in front of me.
>
> "Traveling?" he asked. "Where to? Trusting to

providence?"

"I'm making for Crete. Why do you ask?"

"Taking me with you?"

I looked at him carefully. He had hollow cheeks, a strong jaw, prominent cheekbones, curly gray hair, bright, piercing eyes

"Why? What should I do with you?"

He shrugged his shoulders.

"Why! Why!" he exclaimed with disdain. "Can't a man do anything without a why? Just like that, because he wants to? Well, take me, shall we say, as a cook. I can make soups you've never heard or thought of. … "

—Nikos Kazantsakis, *Zorba the Greek*

Though actions speak louder than words (and are therefore, as evidence goes, far more potentially damning), still, we stand to learn a good deal from characters by the things they say, and by how they are said. Even when their words contradict their actions, we learn something from that contradiction.

And just as action grows out of desire, dialogue grows out of action. *To the extent that characters want things they exist.* Likewise, to the extent that characters, even those as taciturn as Gary Cooper's Will Kane in *High Noon*, must speak to achieve their goals, they will do so.

Here is Jayne Anne Phillips in "1934" evoking the character of father from his son's viewpoint, combining summarized description, generalized action (note the use of the conditional tense), and specific dialogue:

> And I'd walk him downtown. "Frank, my boy,"
> he'd say, and put his arm around me. He'd tip his
> hat to all the women. He was a very handsome
> man, my father. He'd fairly swagger with happi-
> ness, and everyone on the street spoke to him.
> They'd nod and shake hands eagerly, the men
> anxious to talk. At the dry goods store he'd ask
> Mrs. Carvey about her children.
>   "How's Bill doing in the sand lots? That boy
> has a genuine pitcher's arm, Miranda, he should
> be training, it's a fact."

In the above passage Phillips moves, or appears to move, deftly from general to specific. I say "appears to" since a literal reading ("he'd ask") requires us to believe that this man spoke the same dialogue each time he visited the dry goods store. We know better, and take this to be a representative sample of the *type of thing* he'd typically say. As a rule it's best to steer clear of the generalized or conditional (he *would* do such-and-such) in favor of a particular moment or scene (he *does* or *did* such-and-such), since generalized behavior can never pack the punch of a unique occurrence. Then again, as in the example above, conditional and specific can and often are combined to good effect.

I will have more to say about dialogue and its role in evoking character later. Suffice it to say for now that when characters speak we listen less to what they have to say than to how they say it. The Zorba who says "Would you mind, please, taking me to Crete with you?" is not the Zorba I know and love.

We also learn a lot about a character through what **oth-**

er characters have to say, a tactic put to very clever use by Graham Green in his novel *A Burnt-Out Case:*

> "What are they singing [the passenger asked the captain after dinner]? What kind of song? A love song?"
>
> "No," the captain said, "not a love song. They sing only about what has happened during the day, how at the last village they bought some fine cooking-pots which they will sell for a good profit farther up the river, and of course they sing of you and me."
>
> "What do they sing about me?"
>
> "They are singing now, I think." He put the dice and counters away and listened.
>
> "Shall I translate for you? It is not altogether complimentary."
>
> "Yes, if you please."
>
> "'Here is a white man who is neither a father nor a doctor. He has no beard. He comes from a long way away—we do not know from where—and he tells no one to what place he is going nor why. He is a rich man, for he drinks whisky every evening and he smokes all the time. Yet he offers no man a cigarette.'"

To be sure, when characters speak of other characters, we shouldn't always accept what they say at face value; we have to take what they say with a grain or two of salt, or at least with the understanding that their views may not be objective. Still, their testimonies are added to what amounts to a thick mental dossier in which the reader gathers evidence from all of the above-mentioned sources, and possibly from other sources as well.

Depending on the type of narrative you're creating, you may wish to add to your reader's dossier a character's own internal thoughts, also sometimes called interior monologue or stream-of-consciousness. These may come in the third person, as here:

> What a lark! What a plunge! For so it had always seemed to her when, with a little squeak of the hinges, which she could hear now, she had burst open the French windows and plunged at Bourton into the open air. How fresh, how calm, stiller than this of course, the air was in the early morning; like the flap of a wave; chill and sharp and yet. ...
> —Virginia Woolf, *To the Lighthouse*

Note than when conveying a character's thoughts in the third person you needn't set them in quotation marks, or italicize them, as some authors do—annoyingly, in my opinion, since such devices are not only an eyesore, but insult the reader's intelligence by assuming that he needs the tip-off. And anyway thoughts aren't quotable, since most people don't even think in words, let alone in complete sentences. We use words to replicate thoughts because we have no choice; we are writers; words are our medium. But putting them in quotation marks calls undue attention to them.

Of course, a first-person narrator can also convey her own thoughts directly to the reader:

> If you really want to know about it, the first thing you'll probably want to know is where I was born, and what my lousy childhood was like, and

how my parents were occupied and all before
they had me, and all that David Copperfield kind
of crap, but I don't feel like getting into it, if you
want to know the truth.
     —J. D. Salinger, *The Catcher in the Rye*

Call me Ishmael. Some years ago—never mind
how long precisely—having little or no money in
my purse, and nothing in particular to interest me
on shore, I thought I would sail about a little and
see the watery part of the world. ...
     —Herman Melville, *Moby-Dick*

Each of these methods works in combination with the
others, and all have their advantages. But the bald short-
hand of summary can never hope to paint as clear, solid
and convincing a portrait as a moving image (action) or a
soundtrack (dialogue)—let alone both combined. Forced to
establish a hierarchy for these methods, I would say that action speaks more loudly than dialogue, which speaks more
loudly than thoughts, which speak more loudly than physical descriptions, which speak louder then epithets.

But no one is forcing us to choose one method over
another. In fact we can choose them all, in whatever combinations best suit our purposes. There's a time to show and a
time to tell, a time for scene and a time for summary, a time
for action and a time for description. . .

I'll stop there, lest you assume that you've stumbled into
chapter 3 of Ecclesiastes.

7. NAMES

Names tell us as much about a character as the other things I've listed above. Sally Bowles, Bigger Thomas, Augie March, Ignatius O'Reilly ... The Manhattan white pages is as good a source for names as any. Whatever names you choose for your characters, they should feel right. And even if they are your narrators, and their names appear nowhere in their stories, still, you should name your main characters, since you can't possibly know them and not know their names.

In naming characters, you sometimes need to walk a thin line between the memorable and the outrageous. From someone named Joe Smith or Martha Jones I expect little wit or originality. On the other hand a character named Sebastian Dangerfield—the protagonist of J.P. Donleavy's *The Ginger Man*—promises to be a handful, and delivers. However many decades go by, Miss Jane Brodie will forever be in her prime, since I equate her name with an eternally vain and self-deceiving woman. John Kennedy Toole's Ignatius O'Reilly *(A Confederacy of Dunces)* is one character whose name I won't soon forget, because I find it so implausible. As for Scarlet O'Hara, her name alone—with its traces of blood and blarney—makes her memorable.

Yet a character name need not be sensational or even extraordinary to burn itself into our brains. Randall Patrick ("R.P.") McMurphy is an ordinary but memorable name. So is Elizabeth Bennet. Yet we remember these names as we do the names of people we grew up or went to school with, since their stories touch us like our own.

CHAPTER II:
POINT OF VIEW

"No point of view, no story."

II. POINT OF VIEW

In real life, events can be—and often are—experienced by more than one person. So too with fictional events, in which case each character will have a different perspective on those events. It's up to us to decide which perspective or perspectives to convey to our readers, whether to convey one viewpoint only, or more than one, or to alternate between several viewpoints. Or to tell the story from an all-seeing, godlike vantage point.

I've put this lesson second because I think point of view is one of the most fundamental elements of the fiction writing craft, and also the most daunting and misunderstood. Arguably, the choice of viewpoints is the most crucial one we have to make. More than anything else, it will determine our readers' responses to the plights of our characters, turning sympathies for or against them, and governing not only what readers feel, but how deep those feelings run.

The story of an adulterous affair affects us very differently when told from the point of view of the cuckolded husband, as opposed to that of the unfaithful wife or her lover. Described from the point of view of the adulterer's brother, or some neutral or peripheral party, the story is transformed again, changing its colors like a fox changing the colors of its coat.

Who's story is it? From whose point of view is it being told? The answers to both questions may be the same, or they may not. But we writers should have the answers.

1. TYPES OF POINT OF VIEW: FIRST PERSON

As writers, we have too many options. We may tell our stories in the first person, from the point of view of our protagonists, on their authority and in their own words, as Scott Spencer does in *Endless Love*, his novel about a boy who literally goes crazy over a girl:

> When I was seventeen and in full obedience to my heart's most urgent commands, I stepped far from the pathway of normal life and in a moment's time ruined everything I loved—I loved so deeply, and when that love was interrupted, when the incorporeal body of love shrank back in terror and my own body was locked away, it was hard for others to believe that a life so new could suffer so irrevocably. But now, years have passed and the night of August 12, 1967, still divides my life.

Here you have the start of a journey to madness and back straight from the mad hero's mouth. There's great urgency in the telling, also intimacy and immediacy, despite that years have passed since the crucial events took place. We listen with pricked ears, knowing we are getting the inside scoop. This is a first-person "I" point of view, but by no means the only type of "I" viewpoint. There are others.

> My father is eighty-six years old and in bed. His heart, that bloody motor, is equally old and will not do certain jobs any more. It still floods his head with brainy light. But it won't let his legs carry the weight of his body around the house.
> —Grace Paley, "A Conversation With My Father"

Here, we're still in a first-person narrative, since a character in the story is telling the story. But the narrator is no longer the focus of the story; her father is. We call this type of narrator a *peripheral* narrator. Under the right circumstances, a peripheral narrator can have many benefits. In a story where your protagonist lacks all objectivity—is hysterical, in fact—your peripheral narrator can be calm and objective; while the hero (or antihero) of your story may be an imbecile, your peripheral narrator can be a genius—or articulate, at least. We get all the intimacy of a first-person narrative, combined with the objectivity, intelligence, analysis, and perspective normally reserved for omniscient narrators (see below).

Let's go back to *Moby-Dick*, and Ishmael—possibly the most famous of all peripheral narrators. In the unlikely event that it's not already scrimshawed into your psyche, here's the opening:

> Call me Ishmael. Some years ago—never mind how long precisely—having little or no money

> in my purse, and nothing in particular to interest
> me on shore, I thought I would sail about a little
> and see the watery part of the world. ...

Why does Melville choose to tell us his story through the eyes of a contract seaman—whose role in the drama is relatively insignificant—rather than through, say, the eyes of Captain Ahab, or Moby Dick? For good reasons. First, because whales don't talk (though I suppose Melville could have gotten around that). But also because the white whale isn't privy to most of what happens aboard the *Pequod*, where nearly all of the story's dramatic events take place, including most of Ahab's stormy harangues.

Why not have Ahab himself tell his tale? For a start because he's mad, and we can't take at face value things a madman tells us; we must swallow them with a few gallons of seawater, and maybe a Tylenol or two. Told by Ahab, *Moby-Dick* would be a tale of dementia in the words of a senile loon whittling his way to oblivion on the front porch of the Home for Retired Sailors.

But the strongest reason for having Ishmael narrate *Moby-Dick* is because, as Ishmael himself tells us through Job, "And I only am escaped alone to tell thee." Except for the whale, the rest of the cast all die, and the dead (usually) don't speak.

The ideal peripheral narrator is charming, personable, articulate, philosophical, poetic, with ample access to the principal characters during crucial moments in their lives. Remember Gatsby flinging his shirts for Daisy? There was Nick Carraway, our narrator, right there in the bedroom with them. The peripheral narrator has no axes to grind, no ulterior motives beyond telling a story as best he can with the materials available to him.

But even when a peripheral narrator has all these good qualities, he still has two great drawbacks: he can't be in more than once place at a time (a drawback shared by all narrators lacking omniscience); and he can't report directly what he hasn't witnessed first hand.

This second drawback is one authors often get around by cheating, as Melville does shamelessly in *Moby-Dick* (then again what doesn't Melville do shamelessly in *Moby-Dick?*), having Ishmael narrate for us in vivid detail scenes and moments at which he was not present. Authors often excuse such tactics by having the narrator explain that he has learned of the events from another party, but this does little to justify to vividness of the recreation. Cheat a little, by all means, if you must. But if you find yourself cheating constantly you may need to fire your peripheral narrator and hire someone who can do the job properly.

2. UNRELIABLE (FIRST PERSON) NARRATORS

Here's another, less common type of first-person narrator:

> I made my exit, and it was not until after I had done so that it occurred to me I had not actually offered my condolences (on the death of my assistant, Miss Kenton's, aunt). I could well imagine the blow the news would be to her, her aunt having been, to all intents and purposes, like a mother to her, and I paused out in the corridor, wondering if I should go back, knock and

> make good my omission. But then it occurred to
> me that if I were to do so, I might easily intrude
> upon her private grief.
> —Kazuo Ishiguro, *The Remains of the Day*

We call this type of narrator unreliable not because he plays loose with the facts (he doesn't), but because he fails to grasp what those facts reveal. Though he tells the story accurately, he doesn't understand the story that he's telling. That the butler narrator of Ishiguro's novel is in love with his assistant, Miss Kenton, is plain enough for us, the readers, to see. But the butler can't see it. He's so used to masking his feelings out of a warped sense of protocol and decorum he's lost touch with them completely.

All first-person narrators, from Huck Finn to Holden Caufield, are *somewhat* unreliable, since their views are distorted by the intensity and subjectivity of their emotions. Still, there's a big difference between a *subjective* narrative and an *unreliable* one. The difference being this: that the subject of a story told by an unreliable narrator is always the narrator's unreliability. If you create an unreliable narrator, know that you've done so, and why. His unreliability should be intentional, not accidental or incidental.

For other famous examples of unreliable narrators see Ford Maddox Ford's *The Good Soldier*, Nabokov's *Lolita*, and the short story, "Goodbye, My Brother," by John Cheever.

3. ADVANTAGES & DISADVANTAGES OF FIRST PERSON

A character telling his or her own or another character's story is never wholly objective, yet—except in the exotic case of an unreliable narrator—we trust that what they're telling us is essentially and emotionally true. Because it carries subjective content, a first-person narrative can be pitched emotionally higher than any other viewpoint; it can read like a confession ripped from the heart, or an accusation drawn like a dagger. To reach those high, fevered notes in stories like "The Tell-Tale Heart," Edgar Allen Poe used the first person.

But there are disadvantages. As already mentioned, the first-person narrator can only report on events he or she has witnessed or overheard; the rest are off-limits. Often these knowledge gaps can help build suspense by providing legitimate excuses for withholding information. Such restrictions test a writer's skills, while steering him toward characters who are in the habit of eavesdropping.

In a first-person narrative, convention allows a narrator to speak almost as well as his or her author, despite being eight years old:

> When he was nearly thirteen, my brother Jem got his arm badly broken at the elbow. When it healed, and Jem's fears of never being able to play football were assuaged he was seldom self-conscious about his injury. His left arm was somewhat shorter than his right; when he stood or walked, the back of his hand was at right angles to his body, his thumb parallel to his thigh. He couldn't have cared less, so long as he could pass and punt.
> —Harper Lee, *To Kill a Mockingbird*

How many eight year-olds on your block say "assuaged"? And yet most readers accept this word coming from Scout Finch's lips because convention lets them do so. It also allows us to believe that in *A Farewell to Arms* Frederick Henry can tell a story just as well as Ernest Hemingway (while spelling his Italian just as badly), and that *Great Expectation's* Pip can write as well as Dickens. Our tendency to accept in fiction what we would not in real life is called willing suspension of disbelief, but it only goes so far. Were Pip to stud his narrative, as Melville might have, with compound sentences and ponderous Latinate words, we wouldn't for a minute buy it.[1] The same viewpoint that lets an author write the way her characters talk also *obliges* her to do so, more or less. If your narrator lays bricks for a living, he should sound more like James Jones or Henry Miller than like Henry James.

If (on the other hand) the limits of a character's insights or vocabulary are inadequate to the tale being told, if he or she can't do the job, you may want to consider firing them and hiring someone who can. Or switch to third person, or to an anonymous omniscient narrator.

A last word about first person: As Leon Surmelian has observed, it's "better for the sinner than for the saint." For obvious reasons, we're much more likely to take the sinner at his word. Céline's *Journey to the End of the Night* is narrated in the first person by a scoundrel; told in the third person, it would lose much of its power. That being so, wouldn't Dostoevsky's *Crime and Punishment* have been better in first person? Well, Dostoevsky didn't think so.

1 My twin brother George for one feels that Melville's heavy use of Latinisms for his narrator in *Moby-Dick* is contrived and absurd.

Sometimes we want our narratives to be whipped to a froth by the emotions of our main characters as they in turn are whipped about by the storm of events. Sometimes we find an ideal peripheral narrator standing at the calm center—the "I"— of the storm. And sometimes we want to step out of the storm entirely and report it from a safe, objective distance.

4. SECOND PERSON

In the interest of plurality (pun intended) I include this brief mention of second person, though it functions exactly like first person, with a pronoun-change operation. A notorious example:

> You are not the kind of guy who would be at a place like this at this time of the morning. But here you are, and you cannot say that the terrain is entirely unfamiliar, although the details are fuzzy. You are at a nightclub talking to a girl with a shaved head. . .
>
> —Jay McInerney, *Bright Lights, Big City*

The attention-grabbing benefits of this technique are undeniable, and yet it, too, has its drawbacks. Supposing your reader, while reading your story, does not happen to be talking to a girl with a shaved head? In that rare event, said reader may condemn the author's presumption and inaccuracy. He may also resent being forced into the action of your story rather than otherwise compelled. Personally, I find the technique distracting, its novelty thin and short-lived. For this reason it works better with a story or a no-vella like *Bright Lights* than with longer works.

5. THIRD PERSON: SUBJECTIVE AND OBJECTIVE

As complicated as things already are, they get more compli-cated when we turn to third person, and our choices multiply.

The third-person limited subjective point of view tech-nique (see what I mean by complicated?) is almost identical to the first person except that "I" has been replaced by "he" or "she." You're still limiting your viewpoint to single charac-ter, and you're still able to plunge as deeply into that char-acter's subjective thoughts and feelings.

For example, instead of writing, "Sally saw the painting on the wall," you could write, "Oh, what a gorgeous paint-ing! Sally thought." Or:

> Wow, thought Sally, who did this painting? She raised her hand to the canvas, threatening to touch it, holding her fingers stretched there as if to capture the heat exuded by its thick impas-tos and warm colors. She'd never seen anything more lovely. Or was she held captive by her general sense of euphoria, so everything she saw glowed with fresh, spectral light—as if she'd just recovered from cataract surgery?

Third person can be moving and intimate. Listen:

> Now optimistic, Alex grabbed the bauble that must be twisted to open blinds. His fingers were too sweaty. He shuttled up the bed, dried his

left hand on the wall, gripped and pulled. The rain had come in the night. It looked as if the Flood had passed through Mountjoy, scrubbed it clean. The whole place seemed to have undergone an act of accidental restoration. He could see brickwork, newly red-faced and streaky as after a good weep, balconies with their clean crop of wet white socks, shirts and sheets. Shiny black aerials. Oh, it was fine. Collected water had transformed every gutter, every depression in the pavement, into prism puddles. There were rainbows everywhere.

Alex took a minute to admire the gentle sun that kept its mildness even as it escaped a gray ceiling of cloud. On the horizon a spindly church steeple had been etched by a child over a skyline perfectly blue and flatly colored in. To the left of that sat the swollen cupola of a mosque, described with more skill. So people were off to see God, then, this morning. All of that was still happening. Alex smiled, weakly. He wished them well.

—Zadie Smith, *The Autograph Man*

Here we are firmly planted in Alex's head—in his skin, even—distanced from him only by the use of the third-person pronoun, a semantic distance, mainly, though one that also allows us to momentarily step far enough out of his viewpoint to see him smile, weakly.

When to use third-person limited subjective over first person? The choice is a fine one, and comes down to greater flexibility of diction and psychic distance (how deeply immersed we are in a character's thoughts at any given moment) on the one hand (third person), and a sense of authenticity and intimacy on the other (first person). Again, these are not mutually exclusive properties. In the hands of a capable author both techniques may share any and all of them.

With the third-person limited objective point of view, the narrative doesn't enter the mind of the character it limits itself to. This is an icy, literal, cinematic technique. As with a movie, we hear all the dialogue, witness events, observe settings often in great detail. But as with Hemingway's story "The Killers," we can only guess at what characters are thinking and feeling:

> The door to Henry's lunchroom opened and two men came in. They sat down at the counter. … Outside it was getting dark. The street light came on outside the window. … The two of them went out the door. George watched them through the window, pass under the arc light and across the street. In their light overcoats and derby hats they looked like a vaudeville team. George went back through the swinging door into the kitchen and untied Nick and the cook. … Nick went up the street beside the car tracks and turned at the next arc light down a side street. Three houses up was Hirsch's rooming house. Nick walked up two steps and pushed the bell. … Nick opened the door and went into the room. Ole Andersen was lying on the bed with his clothes on.

An interesting technique, but one with its own severe limitations. Through it the author—like a filmmaker—must convey everything concretely, through action and dialogue. As techniques go it's stark, cold-blooded, brutal—just like Hemingway's story. The reader's emotions are engaged viscerally, through the senses, or not at all. The objective technique has no time for poetry, explanations, or ruminations: just (as Kerouac said) "what is." The overall effect is like being whacked repeatedly with a blunt object. First it stings, but after a while you go numb. Which is why as techniques go the third-person objective is best for short, blunt, visceral stories dominated by action and dialogue. Of such a technique Hemingway is the hands-down master.

But most third-person narratives, whether limited or divided among several characters (which method I'll attend to shortly), are *subjective:* They let us in on the characters' thoughts and feelings.

Here's another example:

> She pulled off the road. I should go back and see what I've done, she thought. She turned the motor off. She felt she was still moving, and the road shifted into three levels. Wet grass of the road banks was lush. The road shimmered; one plane of it tilted and moved sideways into the other. Jancy gripped the vinyl seat of the car.
> —Jayne Anne Phillips, "The Heavenly Animal"

Notice how Philips slides in and out of her character's stream of conscience, how she dispenses with quotation marks for thoughts, since thoughts are not spoken, and how, by loosening up her grammar and working with sentence fragments ("Wet grass of the road banks was lush") she replicates the fragmentary thoughts of a somewhat perturbed mind. For an example of this technique on steroids and expanded to eight hundred pages, read—or just dip into—James Joyce's *Ulysses*.

Subjectivity is wanted in any narrative in which characters' hidden thoughts or feelings are a crucial part of the story. And since they are a crucial part of *most* stories, most stories are narrated with some degree of subjectivity.

6. Limited vs. Serial Viewpoints

Both first-person and third-person narratives can be limited in scope to one character's viewpoint, or divided among a series of characters, with the point of view fluctuating scene to scene, chapter to chapter, or—and this is a bit trickier—from paragraph to paragraph, with the same scene told from two or more viewpoints.

This last technique verges on and is often confused with the *omniscient* technique. But with omniscience there are absolutely no limits on the viewpoints available to the author at any given moment in her narrative (such that, if she wants to, she can narrate part of a scene from the viewpoint of a fly on the wall or the wall itself), whereas with serial third person she has to pick and choose from among a select few characters—rarely more than two per scene—and always be in one or another character's head. Usually, though, with serial third person, transitions from one viewpoint to another are clearly indicated by chapter breaks, white spaces, or some other formatting device.

Even so, the line between a serial, subjective third-person narrative and one that is truly omniscient can indeed be fine or blurry. In *As I Lay Dying*, William Faulkner switches between fifteen narrators (including a gang of pallbearers and the corpse *in* the coffin) fifty-one times in two-hundred and fifty pages!

7. OMNISCIENCE

Like first person, the third-person technique, whether limited or applied serially to more than one character, locks the reader into one viewpoint at a time. It narrows perspective while making a godlike world view impossible. For this reason Henry James called it barbaric.

With both third and first person, there is no godlike, all-seeing, overarching viewpoint, no one to tell us, in no uncertain terms, how the world works. True, with a third- or even a first-person narrator we may get objectivity; we may even get philosophy (usually the author's). As Fitzgerald wrote, "How anyone can take up the responsibility of being a novelist without a sharp and concise attitude about life is a puzzle to me."

But except when dispensed by an omniscient narrator, that "sharp and concise attitude about life" is limited to the conscience of a single human being, one who doesn't see (and therefore can't know) all; whose perspectives limit his objectivity.

Third-person narrators are only human, after all. They may have a broad view of things, but not the broadest possible view.

Omniscience, then, affords us the broadest of all possible views: the ability not only to see widely and clearly, but with X-ray vision, through superficial actions and motivations to the underlying forces that determine them.

Omniscience knows no limitations. It can be in two rooms at once, or even three. It can know what two characters are thinking and feeling as they argue or make love. It can provide us with the perspective of a bird, or a cauliflower, if it wants to. It is the author as god, animating everything he creates. When a story's viewpoint is omniscient we see the action through this all-seeing god's penetrating eyes—with those eyes moving from earth to cloud as need be, seeing from a distance, but also, as the situation merits, up close, from within various characters' minds.

Occasionally this authorial "god" comes to us, like the gods of antiquity, disguised as a mere mortal, often as the author himself, and may even refer to himself in the first person. Don't be confused: it may *sound* like the author (or some other unnamed person) talking to us. But it's an omniscient narrator—a *persona* adopted by the author who is much closer to god than the author himself.

The omniscient narrator has the greatest range of movement and psychological and linguistic freedom, but at the potential expense of authenticity, intimacy, and grit. Whether you believe in the Almighty or not, it's harder to believe in an unlimited viewpoint than in a limited one. But then it doesn't matter, really, since the act of reading fiction involves a fundamental suspension of disbelief—enough suspension, anyway, to justify the existence of omniscient narrators.

Which explains why many if not most of the world's

greatest narratives are written using the omniscient point of view: Hugo's *Les Miserables*, Flaubert's *Madame Bovary*, Tolstoy's *War and Peace*. But that's deceptive, since most of the world's great stories were written in times past, and with the times techniques have changed. These days omniscience has fallen out of favor. Why? Blame Nietzsche, if you like. Or blame the movies, which handle epic and spectacle so well—better than most authors *(The Bridge on the River Kwai* is a far better movie than book). True, movies don't let us enter the minds of their characters. But to do that you don't need God or omniscience. First or third person will do.

Still, it's impossible and frankly wrong to completely overlook the strengths of the omniscient approach. For one thing it lets authors, in their own shameless voices, amuse us and themselves, as Henry Fielding did to a turn in *Tom Jones:*

> Reader, I think proper, before we proceed any further together, to acquaint these that I intend to digress, through this whole history, as often as I see occasion, of which I am myself a better judge than any pitiful critic whatsoever; and here I must desire those critics to mind their own business. …
>
> I have told my reader, in the proceeding chapter, that Mr. Allworthy inherited a large fortune. …

The same sort of authorial brio consumes so much of Lawrence Sterne's energies that he digresses his way through all of *Tristram Shandy*, so much so that it takes four volumes for his title character to be conceived, and two more for him to be breeched. Sterne is so enamored of his own authorial license that his preface appears three volumes into his book, a dedication is hawked to the highest bidder among his readers, and at one point he offers us his backside in the form of a page blackened with ink. Which, depending on one's mood, is either very funny or reader abuse.

If the omniscient narrator is godlike, then the above are examples of gods gone power-hungry and mad. But an omniscient god needn't be either. He may be benign, beneficial, or sublime, like the narrator of Giuseppe di Lampedusa's *The Leopard:*

> Now, as the voices fell silent, everything dropped back into its usual order or disorder. Benedicto, the Great Dane, grieved at exclusion, came wagging its tail through the door by which the servants had left. The women rose slowly to their feet, their oscillating skirts as they withdrew baring bit by bit the naked figures from mythology painted all over the milky depths of the tiles. Only an Andromeda remained covered by the soutane of Father Pirrone, still deep in extra prayer, and it was some time before she could sight the silvery Perseus swooping down to her aid and her kiss.

Here omniscience allows di Lampedusa to enter the mind not only of a dog, but of a mythological figure painted into the floor tiles of the Sicilian villa in which his story is set— all in a paragraph. This, too, would seem to be omniscience carried to an extreme. Yet in the context of the novel it calls no undue attention to itself, and goes down like good wine.

Here is Hannah Tinti exercising true omniscience in her story "Home Sweet Home":

> It was a warm spring evening full of summer

promises. Pat and Clyde's bodies lay silent and
still while the orange sunset crossed the floors
of their house and the streetlights clicked on. As
darkness came and the skunks waddled through
the backyard and the racoons crawled down
from the trees, they were still there, holding their
places, suspended in a moment of quiet blue before the sun came up and a new day started and
life went on without them.

Such is the beauty of the omniscient POV: it sees all,
knows all, can move like a fly buzzing around a kitchen, or
a town, around the whole world, if need be. The result is
still a report, one that's by and large impersonal, or only as
personal as the characters and their individual thoughts—
which are presented to us as part of the report.

The great instigator and master of the *impersonal* omniscient style (as opposed to the deeply personal styles of the
eccentric narrators in Fielding and Sterne) is Flaubert, with
Madame Bovary that style's exemplar. As Flaubert himself
put it, "The author should be felt everywhere, and visible
nowhere." That's as good a summing up of the impersonal
omniscient approach as we're likely to get. In Chekhov's
short stories, he, too, observes this dictum, never stopping
to preach or editorialize or otherwise chat with his readers.

To repeat, the main disadvantage of the omniscient
point of view is that it can seem old-fashioned. It can also
seem cheeky, false, controlling, preachy, or distant and impersonal. But in the hands of a master it can wipe the floor
with all other techniques. Listen to Private Robert E. Lee

Prewitt blowing taps at dusk:

> This is the song of the men who have no place,
> played by a man who has never had a place, and
> can therefore play it. Listen to it. You know this
> song, remember? This is the song you close your
> ears to every night, so you can sleep. This is the
> song you drink five martinis every evening not to
> hear. This is the song of the Great Loneliness that
> creeps in like the desert wind and dehydrates
> the soul. This is the song you'll listen to on the
> day you die. When you lay there in the bed and
> sweat it out, and know that all the doctors and
> nurses and weeping friends dont mean a thing
> and cant help you any, cant save you one small
> bitter taste of it, because you are the one thats
> dying and not them; when you wait for it to
> come and know that sleep will not evade it and
> martinis will not put it off and conversation will
> not circumvent it and hobbies will not help you
> to escape it; then you will hear this song and,
> remembering, recognize it. This song is reality.
> Remember?
> —James Jones, *From Here to Eternity*

Try doing *that* in first or third person.

8. TENSE

I've tucked tense into this discussion of point of view since, like our choice of viewpoint, the choice of tense—past or present—significantly alters the tone of anything we write.

Chapter II

Like first person, the present tense is more immediate, allowing for little if any perspective with respect to the long-range consequences of events described.

> I am in the basement sorting clothes, whites with whites, colors with colors, delicates with delicates—it's a segregated world—when my youngest child yells down the steps. She yells when I'm in the basement, always, angrily, as if I've slipped below the surface and though she's twenty-one years old she can't believe it.
> —Jayne Anne Phillips, "Something that Happened"

Like movies and plays, present-tense narratives are permeated with the sense of *now*. Each moment is rendered sharp as a knife, and we feel its blade slicing into us as we read. Present and past tense differ as much as a headache you suffered a year ago differs from the one you feel now, today. The effect of present tense is immediate and visceral, or can be, if the events described are likewise immediate and visceral.

But used to convey general, inert information the present tense can be deadening, if not deadly. Converted to present tense, even the opening of *The Chosen*, Chaim Potok's greatest novel, sounds awkward and dull:

> For more than fifteen years, Danny and I live within five blocks of each other and neither of us knows of the other's existence. ...
> Danny's block is heavily populated by the

> followers of his father, Russian Hasidic Jews in
> somber garb, whose habits and frames of refer-
> ence are born on the soil of the land they have
> abandoned.

Here the present tense swallows any sense of historical perspective, replacing it with an ersatz immediacy unearned by the content itself. For this reason present tense should never be used arbitrarily or in an effort to inject a work not otherwise suited for it with a contemporary cinematic style. Besides, having been in heavy use since John Updike used it in 1960 for the first of his Rabbit novels, present tense is no longer a novelty. If anything it has grown stale from overuse.[2]

Past tense allows for greater perspective (see the opening paragraph of *Endless Love* at the beginning of the chapter), while charging the narrative with a certain *fait accompli* authority, since it's given that there is a story to be told. With present tense the fictional ground that we stand on isn't as solid; the impact of the future remains to be seen.

Which to choose? For material endowed with intrinsic immediacy, when what matters is what's happening *right now,* you might try present tense. Cinematic stories, stories told chiefly through action and dialogue, dramatically,

---

2 For an extended discussion on the present tense and its drawbacks read William H. Gass's "A Failing Grade for the Present Tense," originally published in the October 11, 1987 issue of *The New York Times Book Review*, in which he says, "Why do I warn you about the perils of the present tense? Because there is a lot of it going around. What was once a rather rare disease has become an epidemic. In conjunction with the first person, in collusion with the declarative mode, in company with stammery elisions and verbal reticence—each often illnesses in their own right—it has become that major social and artistic malaise called minimalism, itself a misnomer."

often work well in present tense. Again, try it. If it doesn't work, or if you're not sure and want to err on the side of caution, stick to the past tense, which has been and will go on being the gold standard for telling stories.

9. POINT OF VIEW: PLANNING AND CONSISTENCY

"If you violate the point of view, you destroy the, sense of reality and louse yourself up generally."
—Flannery O'Connor

When he first tried to write what would become *One Flew Over the Cuckoo's Nest,* his greatest novel, Ken Kesey couldn't get a handle on his material. He'd worked briefly as an attendant on a mental ward, and had his plot and characters down cold. Still, the thing wouldn't gel. Then one day, under the influence of peyote or whatever drug he happened to be taking at the time, like a burning bush the solution came to him: Chief Bromden (or Chief "Broom"), the half-Indian schizophrenic who pretends to be deaf and mute while endlessly pushing a broom, would tell the story of R.P. McMurphy; he'd be Kesey's peripheral narrator, seeing and knowing all through his broom-pushing days.

The above anecdote isn't offered to promote the creative benefits of peyote, but to get you to see how important your choice of point of view can be. *No point of view, no story.*

Whatever point of view you choose, it pays to be consistent. It may be the hobgoblin of little minds, but when it comes to writing fiction, consistency lets you get away with a lot. Do something more than once and with a purpose and a plan, and no matter how novel or outrageous it is, readers will tend to give you the benefit of the doubt and accept. Do things accidentally and randomly, and they won't let you get away with anything.

When shifting between multiple points of view try not to confuse or make your readers dizzy by hopping around too much. It helps, too, to provide a visual clue—a white space or a chapter break—to let them know you're switching gears. Above all you yourself must be aware, at any given point in your stories, of whose head (or heads) the story is imbedded in. Choose your method and stick to it. Violate it and you'll perplex readers, or enrage them.

Finally, if you do write an omniscient narrative, make sure that you've done so by choice, and not by default.

CHAPTER III:
STRUCTURE AND PLOT

"As regards plot I find real life no help at all. Real life seems to have no plots. And as I think a plot desirable and almost necessary, I have this extra grudge against life."
—Francis Bacon

III. STRUCTURE AND PLOT

1. ORDER FROM CHAOS

I write fiction for the same reason some people believe in God, to give meaning and order to life, or at least give it some shape here and there. I'm uncomfortable with chaos and disorder. The studio in which I write contains a medley of tidily arranged shelves, bookcases and surfaces, jars bristling with writing implements, and notebooks arranged by size, shape, category, and date—all within arm's reach. I'm pathologically tidy. But I'm far from alone. For damning evidence of man's fixation with order look no further than heaven. What are the constellations but tidy boxes in which we've shelved the stars? The Big Dipper is cosmic fiction.

Lives are messy things, events loosely (if at all) related, some momentous, most trivial, beads strung along the thread of time. We dig through the pile of events, hoping to unearth a solid premise or theme or any hint of meaning, and end up with a handful of irrelevant details and endless digressions. When death finally ties its tidy little bow on the clutter it usually does so too early, or too late, and for no good reason at all.

Lives tend to be shapeless. And what has no shape has no meaning, or doesn't seem to have any.

> *"To find the form that accommodates the mess,*
> *that is the task of the artist now."*—Beckett

To the shapeless chaos of life the fiction writer brings order. An alchemist, he turns lead into gold, paste into diamonds. Life supplies the raw materials, but they must be hammered, distilled, molded, carved, sorted—alchemized—into significant form.

To be an alchemist takes skill, cunning, and a hefty dose of dissident faith. Turning lead to gold isn't easy. If you end up with aluminum or bronze, feel lucky.

Often we start with characters, feelings, ideas, and events drawn from our own lives. But that's just the beginning. Aside from there being too much material, the problem with real life as fiction is that the causal linkage between incidents is missing or obscure. In real life things simply happen: an abscess forms under a tooth, blooms into a staff infection, and Cousin Brett dies; the front yard oak, struck by lightning during a storm, lands on your neighbor's prize Airedale, and a feud ignites; the apartment down the hall is robbed, its occupants—who turn out to be narcotics dealers—are murdered; you meet your future bride while trapped in an elevator during a blackout. Such events are certainly fodder for fiction, but only after they've been endowed with that "inner-connectedness" that only dimly exists in everyday life—but which, in fiction, however quietly hidden under the surface of things, should be constantly felt.

I'm talking about the difference between plot and story, summed up so deftly by E.M. Forster in *Aspects of the Novel*:

> "The King died, and then the Queen died" is a story. "The King died, and then the Queen died of grief," is a plot.

The words *of grief* provide the missing link: the *causal relationship* between two seemingly unrelated events, their innerconnectedness.

Plot: events linked by causation.

Another example: "Gloria colored her hair red. That night, she dined alone." A story. "Embarrassed to have her friends discover that she had dyed her hair, that night Gloria dined alone." A plot. Event and time sequence have been preserved, but a sense of causality overhangs both.

When we talk about plot we're talking about what happens in a story, but with the understanding that, in a work of art, things happen *for a reason.* This is why stories that merely transcribe real-life events, autobiographical experiences, or anecdotes, don't usually have plots. Our lives are plotless. They consist of a series of events and situations not selected or shaped by theme, or motivated and linked by causation.

Well, okay, your life *isn't* plotless. But mine is.

I need to interject a note here. Some authors, John Cheever among them, have said that they don't work with plot, that plot "implies narrative and a lot of crap." They prefer to work (Cheever again) by "inspiration, apprehension, dreams, concepts." No one can doubt Cheever's sincerity or deny his process. But even John Cheever's stories have plots, good ones, too. Whether achieved consciously or otherwise, plot can't be ignored. Or it can, but at great risk of losing readers.

2. SUSPENSE

Plot makes us ask: *What happens next?* It does so by a tactic known as suspense, which comes from the Latin and means literally "to hang or suspend." A story raises questions and answers them, only to have those answers provoke more questions. We read with the expectation—largely a matter of faith—that everything in a story serves a purpose, has some point, that all the questions and answers lead somewhere.

Suspense is greatest when the reader's curiosity combines with worry over the fate of a sympathetic or interesting character, known usually as the protagonist. It can (and often is) be heightened through delaying tactics that frustrate the reader's eagerness to learn what happens next.

Such delaying tactics can take the form of descriptive passages, or subplots and other complications that slow the way toward the main climax. In Thomas Hardy's third novel, *A Pair of Blue Eyes,* as his hero literally dangles from a cliff, the author increases suspense by supplying us with a detailed account of the hero's thoughts as he hangs there. When the stakes are high enough, and the delay is supported by a reader's unwavering curiosity, what might otherwise be a digression or just plain annoying can add to suspense.

There are two kinds of suspense. One is artificial, the other real. Real suspense results from questions that exist not only in the mind of the reader, but for the characters as well. In Richard Wright's *Native Son,* whether the bones

[78]

of the girl Bigger Thomas has murdered and burned in the furnace will be discovered by the police we don't know, and neither does Bigger. Since it is shared by both reader and protagonist, the suspense is genuine, it is real.

Artificial suspense results from artificially withheld information. For instance, let's say the author and protagonist each know damn well that Sally is only eight years old and that the love affair with a handsome French sailor who walks her arm-in-arm through the bazaars of Marrakesh is in fact a fantasy being lived out in front of her vanity mirror. The suspense comes from the reader knowing that something's not quite right with this picture, wondering why, and suspecting (but without sufficient evidence to convict) a fantasy. When at last the reader's suspicions are confirmed by the author springing his surprise on her, the result is more frustrating than satisfying, and often accompanied by an acute urge to wring the author's neck.

Less blatant forms of withheld information infect beginner fiction. We read paragraph after paragraph before learning vital statistics about the characters: their names, occupations, where they live, how old they are, and so on, the notion being that these questions will propel readers anxiously forward, when in fact they're more likely to make us toss the novel or story into the trash can. I for one am not interested in plowing through acres of prose to uncover answers to basic questions that should have been provided within the first few pages. Those questions—and their withheld answers—aren't, or shouldn't be, the point.

Knowing when and how much information to provide is among a writer's biggest challenges. Ask yourself, *What does the reader need to know to fully appreciate what is happening in this moment in the story?* Typically, unless you're writing a mystery, the four W's—who, what, where and when—are best disposed of early, clearing the way for deeper, more intriguing questions like how and why.

Of course, the question you want to raise above all in your readers is *What's going to happen next?* Will Elliot shoot himself or his Scandinavian neighbor (Robert Stone, "Helping")? Will Grandma be hauled off and murdered with the rest of her family (Flannery O'Connor, "A Good Man is Hard to Find")? Will Neddy Merril make his way home through all those swimming pools (John Cheever, "The Swimmer")? Will Dorothy meet the Wizard of Oz, get the ruby slippers, and find her way home?

Exceptions to the rule: mysteries, as mentioned, and stories in which the withheld information casts a long, dark shadow, as in Hemingway's "The Killers," in which we never learn why the two hit-men have come to kill the Swede, or "A Clean, Well-Lighted Place," in which we're never told that the old man is suicidal (though we infer it). In William Faulkner's *Sanctuary,* Popeye's impotence and his brutal rape of Temple Drake are never stated, but teased out through implication for the length of the book. In each of these cases, not only does the withheld information *not* interfere with our understanding and appreciation of those stories, it enhances it.

When doling out information, you needn't do so all at once, in one big clump, as journalists do. In fact it's usually best to dole out information on a need-to-know basis throughout your narrative, keeping readers sufficiently oriented, without overburdening them.

3. PLOT & CHARACTER: CAUSE & EFFECT

The innerconnectedness of things is largely supplied by motivation, that force which drives characters toward their goals. You may recall my saying that to the extent that characters want something, they exist. Following through on this notion, to the extent that characters are motivated they make their own plots.

"If you focus on who the people in your story are," writes Anne Lamott in *Bird by Bird,* "if you sit and write about [those characters] you know, and are getting to know better day by day, something is bound to happen."

Writing from character and motivation precludes doing what many novice (and quite a few experienced) writers do: rounding up characters to serve as pawns in a plot that they have already contrived. However intricately constructed, such plots are bound to feel as wooden and creaky as puppet shows, with a slave-cast of marionettes, their motives supplied by the author who pulls their strings.

The best plots are born of the conflict(s) between characters, or between characters and setting (read Jack London's "To Build a Fire"), with protagonists supplying motivation, and *antagonists*—in the form of another character or characters, society, or setting—or any mixture of those things (J.D. Salinger, *A Catcher in the Rye*)—providing conflict and obstacles. In *The Grapes of Wrath,* the landowners represent the novel's true antagonists, the forces of Darwinian capitalism and greed. Whether embodied by other characters or not, the force or forces interfering with the protagonist's goals may be labeled antagonistic.

"Thou shall not make life easy for thy protagonist." So reads one of the commandments chiseled in stone by screenwriting prophet Robert McKee. It applies to us fiction writers, too. Once the goals of your protagonist have been met, either his *real* problems begin (and he sprouts a whole new set of goals), or your story has ended.

In fiction, ideally, things get worse before they get better, with your plot deepening or growing more complicated before it gets resolved. It's up to us, as authors, to make the most of the events that follow from our protagonists' efforts to achieve their desires, to give shape and substance to those desires in the form of visceral scenes; to select those scenes and arrange them for maximum efficiency and effectiveness; and to make sure, once we have endowed them with wills of their own, that our characters don't run away with our stories, to keep them focused on the themes which they themselves have animated through their desires and actions.

> *Characters make their own demands, but against these pressures the mind of the author goes on urging the demands for continuity and unity of the plot."*
> —R. V. Casill

In case you've not heard it a thousand times, I'll repeat the recipe here: (1) Put your protagonist up a tree; (2) throw rocks at him; (3) get him down. Conflict, development, resolution. Sounds simple, right?

4. STRUCTURE

Yes, and no. As nice as it may be to know that a plot contains those three elements, it would be nicer still to know how they're contained, by what sort of structure? A story with no structure is wine without the glass, no story at all.

In the history of writing workshops, as many recipes and formulas for plot have been advanced as diet pills on late-nite infomercials. Some—like the ABCDE formula—appeal to us enormously with their simplicity; they're as easy, they suggest, as learning your ABCs. I'll spell it out:

A is for ACTION
B is for BACKGROUND
C is for CONFLICT or CLIMAX
D is for DEVELOPMENT or DENOUEMENT
E is for ENDING

Neat, huh? Take that formula into your literary kitchen, add some characters, a little description, throw in some dialogue, and voila: instant, well-plotted story/novel.

Those who try this at home will soon discover the world of difference between creating a solid work of fiction and using Hamburger Helper. Applied to a dozen good stories chosen at random, the template proves quickly useless. True, just about any decent story contains all of those tasty ingredients, but in no particular order or combination. And what good is a recipe when it merely lists the ingredients, but doesn't say how to combine them? Or tells you in such a limiting, one-size-fits-all way?

Still, taken one at a time, we can get somewhere analyzing the ingredients.

Action is what characters do, resulting in those events that make up a story. It can encompass anything from violent physical action—a sword fight, death, or murder—to the act of speaking (dialogue). These days, writers tend to begin their stories with action, with the opening paragraph plopping us right down into the heart of a scene. Having gained our attention dramatically, they then provide the necessary **background** for the action. Once we are oriented, they may then introduce (or, if it's already been established, heighten) the conflict while developing the action, chucking a steady stream of rocks at the protagonist in his tree, preferably in a sequence that increases the stakes while escalating the drama (the stones keep getting bigger). An alternative interpretation of the formula calls for writers to push things toward a singular decisive event or **climax,** and from there through a resolution or **denouement** to the ending.

Development accounts for the bulk of most stories. In *The Wizard of Oz,* Dorothy, the protagonist, wants to get back to Kansas, but many obstacles stand in her way (conflict). Along a yellow brick road she encounters characters and situations that will lead her to the Wizard, and ultimately back to her home. Along the yellow brick road her story is developed.

Climax is the resolution of conflict, the point of no return beyond which the protagonist's fate—good or bad—is secured. Romeo's suicide is the climax of Shakespeare's play not because it's the most dramatic moment, but because it seals his fate and determines the resolution by preventing him and Juliet from ever living happily ever after. Less dramatically, the climactic line in Hemingway's story "Hills Like White Elephants" ("Would you please please please please please please please stop talking?") seals the fate of a young couple who have been sipping drinks at a Spanish train station, debating whether they should proceed to Barcelona to abort their unborn child.

The climax of a story or novel needn't be sensational or even conveyed by means of action or dialogue, but can come in the form of an **epiphany,** a sudden awakening or recognition that changes forever the protagonist's view of his world, and hence his life. Joyce' stories collected in *Dubliners* are famous for their epiphanies. Of these, perhaps the most famous of all is that of the boy in "Araby," who, after failing to secure a gift for his sweetheart at a local bazaar, is consumed by a sense not only of his own vanity but of the futility of all romantic gestures in a vulgar, mercenary world.

So much for the first six letters of the alphabet. Applied to a story like Cheever's "The Swimmer" or Delmore Schwartz's "In Dreams Begin Responsibilities," let alone to novels like Marilynne Robinson's *Housekeeping,* Martin Amis' *Times Arrow,* or Julio Cortàzar's *Hopscotch*—the ABCDE formula quickly fails. It fails because it is too rigid, too pat.

5. A MORE FLEXIBLE FORMULA

What we need is a more universal, less misleading, basis for structuring our stories and novels. Of all those I've encountered, one strikes me as most honest and versatile. It comes to us from Aristotle by way of the American editor and novelist Peter De Vries:

"A beginning, a muddle, and an end."

The best plots are shaped as much or more by intuition than by logic or by any inflexible recipe or formula. To know what happens next in your own stories, you'll want to stand in your character's shoes and follow their needs and desires, and balance these desires against your own authorial instincts and intentions.

Still, stories have to start somewhere. Why not at the beginning, with what is called an inciting incident: an event or circumstance that motivates unprecedented action in a character, that lifts that character's life out of its everyday existence or status quo (context) into a whole new set of circumstances which may endure for minutes, hours, days—or may even change your protagonist's life forever, or end it.

But why go on speaking hypothetically? Allow me, if you will, to use one of my own stories, "El Malecón," to show you what I mean. Since I wrote the story, I know its origins and can relate the structural possibilities and challenges suggested by the raw material, along with my solutions.

6. "El Malecón": Beginning

My story has its genesis in a weeklong trip I took to the Dominican Republic in the late 1990's. While there, I noticed several things in no particular order:

a. in the outskirts of the city, tin shacks clinging to the side of a muddy ravine

b. on the beach, a man selling coconuts from a wheelbarrow, chopping the coconuts with a machete

c. a sugar-cane stand

d. a toothless old man selling peanuts on a bus crowded with teenagers

e. a polished, late-model American convertible parked in the shade of a palm tree, with a set of keys dangling from the ignition

Observation, Juxtaposition, Supposition

You remember the Five Line Game, the game that I used to play with my father, in which I would draw five random lines on a piece of paper, and he would make a drawing of something using them?

By *juxtaposing* them, I tried to incorporate the above five observations into a single unified picture. What if the toothless peanut vendor and the coconut vendor are one? What if he lives in one of those tin shacks? What if, to make ends meet, he also works at his brother-in-law's *jugo de cana stand*? By juxtaposing observations, a fuller, more distinctive picture of a character and his lot in life begins to form: His background or status quo is established, and along with it the context of a story.

But for it to become an actual story something needs to happen, something to shake this character out of his status quo existence and thereby set in motion a series of unprecedented events. One way to do so is through *supposition*, which does for status quo more or less what yeast does to dough.

Supposing the old man chances upon that shiny convertible with the keys in the ignition (or, as it turned out in the final draft, left on the driver's seat)? Supposing he takes it for a spin? With this supposition I had the germ of my story; I had stumbled on my *inciting incident*. I had my beginning.

Here is the opening paragraph of the finished story:

> The car Viva Colon borrowed was a late mod-
> el Cadillac convertible, the paint of which had
> faded to a blue paler than that of the sky. He had
> been walking to his brother-in-law's *yuga de cana*
> stand where he worked when, stopping to rest
> against the trunk of a date palm, he noticed the
> car parked in its shade, and the set of keys gleam-
> ing on its red leather upholstered driver's seat.
> The car was parked about a mile from the bank of
> the river where Viva lived in a rusty tin shack. His
> brother-in-law's red and yellow sugar cane juice
> stand was another two miles away.

Once Viva (my protagonist) gets in that car, starts the engine and drives off, the story, too, is on its way. The next step must be the "muddle": the long section of development leading to conflict, crisis, climax, resolution.

So you would think. But wait. Before setting out on that long journey, it might be best to know where we're headed, or at least to have some idea.

In other words, I looked ahead to the ending: not to what *would* happen, necessarily, but to what I supposed *might* happen, to the broadest possibilities.

7. ENDING

Now comes the time for more speculation. What might happen to an old man with no teeth who gets it into his head to "borrow" a stranger's shiny American car for a joyride? What might he be thinking? What might motivate him? Is he a thief? Doubtful. Then what? Perhaps he's out to impress others? Or maybe he thinks he'll be handsomely rewarded for saving the car from *real* thieves? Or a combination of the above? If he's so determined to impress others, he must be very poor: poor enough to live in one of those sad tin shacks in the ravine. Whom will he impress? Some relatives, perhaps, ones he hasn't seen in some time, years maybe? How will he impress them? By driving up and down their street, honking the horn of his shiny Cadillac (sure, why not make it a Cadillac?), smiling a tight-lipped smile so as not to display his missing teeth.

Now the story has its direction, its thrust. Viva is going to drive to the village where he grew up. With this much information—an old man driving off on a mission in a stolen car—I could certainly begin to write a story (in fact I could have begun with much less and writen on pure faith, by the seat of my pants). But to be sure of what belongs in the "muddle," I followed the trajectory a little further. I imagined this trajectory taking the form of an arrow. What did the arrow point to? Where did the story seem to be headed?

I speculated. What could happen? Would Viva gain his longed-for dignity, win his reward? Or was he bound for a less happy fate? *To the extent that characters want something, they exist.* And to the extent that they encounter obstacles to their desires, stories exist. Ideally, those obstacles will build toward an ultimate obstacle, one which—if conquered—will result in a happy ending; if not, will result in failure and possibly tragedy. This ultimate showdown is what is commonly called the climax of a story.

But I wasn't thinking of that then, at least not in any detail. I was still asking myself broad questions. Will things end well, or badly, for my hero? Will he regain his lost dignity, or wind up in jail, or worse?

My instincts told me that whatever happened in this story, things would not end well for Viva. I felt this in my gut, yet I also understood practically and logically that little good can come from a poor toothless old man stealing someone's Cadillac in a country where the police are known to be brutal and corrupt. In few words, I felt that Viva's story must end badly if not tragically. When writing it pays to honor and obey your instincts.

Now, think of that arrow. It points to the ending, or the likely, *assumed* ending. Let's say that it points to Viva being arrested and thrown in jail. In that case, whatever happens Viva must *not* be arrested and thrown in jail: or, if he is, then it must happen in a way that's unexpected, that doesn't simply fulfill the arrow's prophecy, since in all likelihood your reader will have predicted this very same outcome.

And here is the thing about endings: Though they must be probable, they must never be entirely *predictable*. Ideally, two things should happen when a reader reaches the ends of a story. Her first reaction should be "Oh, my God!" followed in short order by "But of course!" The first reaction is surprise, while the second grows out of a sense of inevitability, the feeling that the story could not possibly have ended any other way.

We should be so lucky that all of our stories always end with surprise and inevitability. Often we're willing to settle for surprise and probability, or even surprise and possibility. What we shouldn't settle for is surprise and impossibility, or predictable inevitability, or probability with no surprise.

That said, the surprise of a good ending doesn't have to be shocking, violent, or in any way sensational. In stories especially, a good ending often resonates with surprise without pulling any sort of "gotcha." What's surprising and inevitable about the ending of Joyce's "The Dead" is the sense of that story opening up to swallow the universe—or, as Caroline Gordon suggested to Flannery O'Connor regarding her endings, "gain[ing] some altitude and get[ting] a larger view." A sense of continuance, that the lives of the characters will keep going, spilling beyond the pages we have read, combined with the sense that what we have read is complete, that nothing more is wanted or needed from the characters or their situations, creates its own quiet inevitability, its own gentle surprise like that of a whispered secret.

8. THE MUDDLE

Having arrived at a vague, provisional ending, you're in a particularly strong position to write the story, leaving yourself lots of elbow room for detail and development, for teasing along the suspense you've initiated, and for all those unexpected moments and occurrences that, with any luck, will take even you, the author, by surprise and make mincemeat of your best-made plans. The best moments in fiction arise from the tension between the author's intentions (the straight arrow) and what grows organically out of the writing process, an action or image that shoots up from the seed (inciting incident) that's been planted in the soil of circumstance (status quo), and which—just when you thought you had it all figured out—alters your character's destiny. That way our stories can truly surprise us. And as Robert Frost said, "No surprise for the writer, no surprise for the reader."

Must you write toward a provisional ending? No. Some authors like to go at it completely blind. Others, like Lawrence Durrell, only look so far ahead. In a *Paris Review* interview, Durrell once said of this approach, "It's like driving a few stakes in the ground; you haven't got to that point in the construction yet, so you run ahead fifty yards, and you plank a stake in to show roughly the direction your road is going, which helps to give you your orientation. But [my stories] are very far from planned in the exact sense."

Back to "our" story: With Viva thus on his way, I considered the things that might fill his journey. When writing the "muddle," remember the five senses: touch, taste, feel, sight, smell. I thought of the sun in his eyes and the wind blowing the thinning strands of his hair. I considered that it may have been years since he was last behind the wheel of a car. When finally he gets the hang of it, how does he sit in the car? Does he look at himself in the rearview mirror? If so, what does he see? What are his thoughts, his fantasies? Along the drive to wherever he thinks he's going, what does the landscape look like? What memories are resurrected? Does he smell the sea air, taste the sugar in the smoke from the processing plant? Does the car radio work? What songs does it play?

> … As he sped along the coast highway, with the white sand beach in plain view through the palm trees to his right, Viva's imagination expanded, and so did his fantasies. He fantasized about all the places, wonderful, beautiful places, that this fine car would take him to, nations and cities of great wealth, some oceans away, others on no map at all except for the one in Viva's head. The possibilities, added to the hot brightness of the sun hitting him square on the cheeks, made him dreamy and dizzy. The next curve brought a squeal of rubber against pavement. Viva's body lurched hard to the left before bolting stiff upright. Having made several swift adjustments, he wrested control back from both car and road again. He drove a little more slowly from then on, with both fists gripping the steering wheel.

All these and more ingredients may be poured into the "muddle," where they not only enrich the story with authenticating details, but help to tease along the suspense aroused in the reader. In my story that suspense takes the form of a simple question: *What will happen to Viva?*

What will happen: Of all the questions you may raise in your readers, that is the best one, since it is the question that keeps readers reading.

Bear in mind, too, that not all stories have simple, dramatic through-lines. In fact most don't. In some superb stories (Cheever's "The Swimmer" springs to mind) the drama is hard to isolate, if it isn't entirely obscure. And yet in such stories, though we may not see it, we *feel* the dramatic tension. Though things may seem calm on the surface, underneath that surface the ground rumbles and shifts, and fates are altered or sealed.

9. MORE ABOUT BEGINNINGS: OPENING LINES

The first words out of an author's mouth can not only determine how the rest of his story is read, but whether it gets read at all. As an editor I admit to being strongly swayed by openings. That doesn't mean that I insist on being grabbed by the throat—a phrase I deplore not just because it's a cliché, but because it suggests that readers respond best to force or violence. It means that within a line or two I can usually tell whether I'm dealing with an artist, a competent hack, or an amateur.

If the beginning of a story is weak, chances are that no one will ever get to the "muddle," let alone to the ending. Though I reject it as the first or ultimate solution, sometimes grabbing readers by the throat works. There's something undeniably gripping about:

> Hale knew they meant to murder him before he had been in Brighton three hours.

or:

> A screaming comes across the sky.

the opening sentences, respectively, of Graham Greene's *Brighton Rock* and Thomas Pynchon's *Gravity's Rainbow*.

Such sentences don't invite so much as drag us into the stories that follow.

But not all readers want to be grabbed by the throat. Some prefer to be gently seduced, in which case a sly wink or a wiggled finger may trump a grappling hook, as with the come-hither opening of Jane Austin's *Pride & Prejudice:*

> It is a truth universally acknowledged, that a single man in possession of a good fortune, must be in want of a wife.

To be amusing, entertaining and interesting you needn't be sensational. Think of yourself as a guest who has just arrived at a dinner party. You wish to make a strong impression. You can pull the tablecloth out from under the settings; that will do it. Or tinkle your wine glass. Or simply begin telling a story in your own beguiling voice, a story filled with charm, eccentricity, and winning details, that takes place in a provocative and/or magical setting. You can hook your tablemates without bruising their necks or abusing the dinnerware.

More good news about beginnings: One can often be achieved simply by amputating a draft's first paragraphs, pages or chapters, or what editors with their infinite tact call "throat-clearing." What's the first interesting thing that happens in my story? Begin there.

Let's look into a few openings, starting with a clunker:

> Dexter was beside himself. His girlfriend, Stella, seemed like she was about to crash and burn.

Chapter III

Were this a leg and I a surgeon, I'd suggest amputation at the hip. There's nothing worth saving here. The first sentence tells me nothing beyond the character's first name and that he is "beside himself"—a cliché, and one rendered useless since we're not told what emotion Dexter is "beside himself" with. Fear? Laughter? The second sentence multiplies the flaws of the first by being longer, and by flaunting an even more flagrant cliché, "crash and burn." Were this the opening of a story submitted to me for my editorial approval, by now I'd have little reason to keep reading, since already I know I'm in the hands of an amateur.

My fellow editors ask me: can you really judge a whole story or novel by its first sentence? No, I can't. But I can judge the quality of the author who wrote it, and based on that judgment keep reading or choose to cut my losses. Such judgments by me are rarely rendered based solely on subject matter or on the events being described. When I first start to read something, I'm not all that interested in plot, much less in being "grabbed" by a sensational scene. What interests me is the particular choice and arrangement of words, and, by extension, the mind behind those choices. I read to learn: *Am I dealing with a genuine writer here, a person with some depth of soul and an ear for language?* Sometimes, to answer that question, a sentence is indeed all it takes.

Let's try another opening.

> He stood at the open doorway wearing his pajamas, frosty air nipping at his toes.

This is better. Still, as I read this author's first words a similar chill passes through me, and I find myself bracing for the next nippy gust. Why? Aside from that "open door-way," the sentence is more or less grammatical; its meaning is clear: a perfectly innocent sentence. Which may be why it leaves me cold: It's *too* innocent; it draws no blood or heat and has no weight or thrust. Unlike "They threw me off the hay truck about noon" (the opening of James M. Caine's *The Postman Always Rings Twice)* or "None of them knew the color of the sky" (Jack London, "The Open Boat"), it augurs nothing, a tip with no iceberg. Also, thanks to its rudimentary positioning in the sentence, buried in its soft center, that "wearing his pajamas," which might have carried some weight, feels inconsequential, while the frost "nipping at his toes" downloads an unintended sound-file of Nat King Cole's warbled vibrato.

Were this not the author's first sentence, and hence presumably his best foot forward, I wouldn't be so hard on it. But it is, and with my expectations for his second-best foot reduced accordingly I read on, but with a frosty heart.

You think I'm being awfully tough on these writers, don't you? But understand that editors get hundreds, even thousands of submissions per year, forcing them to render judgments that are ruthless, if not rash. As writers you—and I—simply can't afford to lead with anything but our best.

Here's the opening of a story submitted recently to the journal I edit:

> One foot through the door and hand raised in greeting, Don Farmer never saw the package coming at him.

CHAPTER III

This has things going for it. It starts right off with action: a man stepping through a door as a package is flung at him. I guess this is what's meant by that trite phrase, grab the reader by the throat, yet the action here isn't gratuitous or violent. The specificity of the character's name is appealing, combining a bland Christian name with a less common surname connoting things agricultural. Will the connotation earn its keep? Or will the name turn out to be ironic? And just what is in that package? Manure? Feed corn? Or nothing at all to do with farming? To find out, I need to keep reading.

If I object to anything in the sentence above it's the awkward, double-decker participle phrase lead-in, which disturbs the chronology of events. (When, exactly, did Don "never" see the package? In hindsight, and not—as the present sentence implies—while stepping through the door.) I'd have started with, "Don Farmer never saw the package coming," stuck in a period, and gone on from there.

These are nitpicks—the kinds of devilish details writers need to look for when revising.

Here are a few winning openers:

> After the plague—it was some sort of Ebola mutation passed from hand to hand and nose to nose like the common cold—life was different.
> —T.C. Boyle, "After the Plague"

> Pat and Clyde were murdered on pot roast night.
> —Hanna Tinti, "Home Sweet Home"

Imagine five or six city blocks could lift, with a
bump, and float away.
   —Jim Shepard, "Love and Hydrogen"

A woman I don't know is boiling tea the Indian
way in my kitchen.
   —Bharati Mukherjee, "The Management
     of Grief"

He believed he was safe.
   —Toni Morrison, *Tar Baby*

There was a boy called Eustace Clarence Scrubb,
and he almost deserved it.
   —C. S. Lewis, *The Voyage of the Dawn
     Treader*

Each of these openers thrusts us, like a spear, into the
body of the story. Each raises a beguiling question: *What
else happened after the plague? How and by whom were Pat
and Clyde murdered? What's five city blocks long and floats?
Who's the tea-making lady? Who is he and why shouldn't he be
safe? Why did Eustace Scrubb almost deserve his name?* Like
an aperitif before a meal these first lines open the reader's
appetite for the stories that follow. They are neither coy nor
obtuse; on the contrary, they are direct and informative—
though the information raises questions.

Too many beginning authors try to tease readers into
stories with impertinent withholding. *Read my story and I'll
tell you my character's name, or what country he's in.* The problem with such a strategy being that to acquire such trivia I

shouldn't have to read a whole bloody story.

A good opening is an invitation. It's the hostess opening the door and stepping aside to reveal the spread. It's not an assault or a brainteaser, but an offering. *Come in and I'll tell you a story.*

10. SOME FINAL THOUGHTS ABOUT BEGINNINGS, MUDDLES, AND ENDINGS

You can write scenes and descriptions out of order, without even knowing precisely what sequence they will fall into ultimately, or if they will even survive to your final draft. The point now, at this early stage, is to discover your own material, to follow in Theodore Roethke's footsteps and learn by going where you must go.

You don't have to begin with the beginning. You can start at the end and double back, or begin *in medias rex*, with the action well underway, then work your way back to the inciting incident and proceed from there through the "muddle" again to the ending, providing necessary background information in bits and pieces as you go.

A word about background information or *back story:* the idea is to keep it to a minimum, to introduce it only once you've earned the reader's attention through suspense, and to measure it out in small doses so that it doesn't bring the action to a dead stop.

Having completed your first draft the question to ask yourself is: Have I judiciously selected the necessary scenes with which to develop my story? If you can tell a story in four scenes, don't tell it in five, or eight. When, in *The Great*

Gatsby, Fitzgerald paints that wonderful scene of Gatsby heaving his silk shirts onto his bed to impress Daisy, he feels no subsequent need to drag us into Gatsby's garage and have him show off his Stutz Bearcat.

With endings, though we may aim straight for a point on the horizon, it's better if we don't get there, exactly. It's also more than likely, since our characters, being motivated, are apt to find their own solutions to their goals and frustrations, which in turn will have their own dramatic consequences. As authors we pull many, but not all, of the strings. Remember, *No surprise in the writer, no surprise in the reader.*

That said, an ending that's surprising but unlikely (if not impossible) isn't satisfying. In both novels and stories the ideal ending is both surprising and inevitable, since a good ending is always the direct result of everything that has come before.

By the same token, an ending that wrests the conflict from the characters and gives it to a tornado, pancreatic cancer, or a runaway bus, won't do. Readers of fiction are interested only in those fates brought about by characters through *their own devices and actions,* and not by random acts of God or public transportation.

The "muddle" is achieved by describing those sensations and situations (actions, thoughts, feelings, etc.) set in motion by the beginning, and through which the protagonist is pulled, as if by an invisible rope, on the way to the ending. And that ending is precipitated by the final, most estimable of a series of impediments to his achieving his goal, otherwise known as the *climax.*

With novels and short stories the situation is similar,

[101]

except that the novelist is running a marathon, while the short story writer is a sprinter.

A final word about plot and structure: Form must always follow and never dictate function. Whatever we're trying to do, whatever motive or madness compels us to do it, that urgency should dictate the shape of our finished works. As the spirit moves us, the form emerges to receive and contain the energy born of that movement. But form itself, no matter how clever or elegant, can never replace what's meant to fill it.

Charles Bukowski said it best:

> *as*
> *the*
> *SPIRIT*
> *wanes*
> *the*
> *FORM*
> *appears*

CHAPTER IV:
DIALOGUE

"All dialogue is between the self and the soul."
—Donald Newlove

IV. DIALOGUE

Intrepid readers, we crawl through deserts of narrative summary, hack our way through rainforests of description, beat paths through weedy meadows of backstory, our throats burning all the while for the cool trickle of human voices, for dialogue.

Readers are born eavesdroppers. As much as we enjoy gossip (and let's face it, most of us do), given a chance we would rather hear things from the source. We long to be the fly on the hospital wall when Frederick Henry, the wounded American ambulance driver, is left alone with Catherine Barkley, his British nurse in Hemingway's *A Farewell to Arms*. When Gregor Samsa wakes up to find himself transformed into a giant beetle, we become beetles ourselves, clinging to the bedpost, waiting to see how his family members will react. Confronted by the murderous Misfit in Flannery O'Connor's *A Good Man in Hard to Find*, each of us, no matter how old, becomes that grandmother.

Dialogue frees us from the stuffy, smoky den of hearsay and conjecture that is exposition, to plop us smack into the middle of the dramatic moment. The writer puts down his narrating pen, his characters speak, and we bend our ears to listen to them.

1. Uses & Abuses of Dialogue

Contrary to what you may think, dialogue's main purpose isn't to advance plot, or to announce, summarize or echo the themes in your stories. It may do these things, too, but they aren't what it does first or best. Dialogue's first task is to *convey character*. To the extent that it does so, it enlightens and entertains. Why is this so? Because (again) fiction is first and foremost about people. And nothing tells us more about people than the things they do. And one thing people do is talk.

Successful dialogue—dialogue that conveys character—is never "realistic" (a word that should always come with quotation marks). Those who've survived the rare torture of reading through a courtroom trial transcript will accept this without further argument. The rest of you, if you want proof, tape record and transcribe a random slice of any *(My Dinner With Andre* being the exception) conversation, and you'll find yourself the unwitting creator of a staccato symphony of hems and haws, pauses, repetitions, stutters, interruptions, dashes and ellipses, with voices tripping and falling all over each other like lobsters in a tank.

Sad but true. The underlying subject of most conversations is the ineptitude of speech as a means of communication. Humans don't speak or listen very well. We're too busy *talking,* and what escapes our lips is mainly the verbal equivalent of mulligan stew.

2. GOOD DIALOGUE: REALISTIC, NO; SPEAKABLE, YES

Though it isn't, really, good dialogue always *seems* "realistic." The great playwrights, from Shakespeare to David Mamet, don't write realistic dialogue. Yet what they do write, however artificial, retains the essential qualities of spoken language and can be reproduced by actors on stage or film so that it sounds conversational.

The same is true, more or less, for dialogue in literature. Listen:

> "My name is Quinn."
>
> "Ah," said Stillman reflectively, nodding his head. "Quinn."
>
> "Yes, Quinn, Q-U-I-N-N."
>
> "I see. Yes, yes, I see. Quinn. Hmmm. Yes. very interesting, Quinn. A most interesting word. Rhymes with twin, does it not?"
>
> "That's right. Twin."
>
> "And sin, too, if I'm not mistaken."
>
> "You're not."
>
> "And also in—one n—or inn—two. Isn't that so?"
>
> "Exactly."
>
> "Hmmm. Very interesting. I see many possibilities for this word, this Quinn, this ... quintessence ... of quiddity. Quick, for example. And quill. And quack. And quirk. ..."
>
> —Paul Auster, *The Invention of Solitude*

Were you to overhear this snatch of dialogue on a bench by the sailboat pond in Central Park, you would assume that the speakers are mad, or that you've gone mad. Or both. Or maybe Paul Auster has gone mad.

But literature isn't life, and so you accept Auster's heavily stylized dialogue as the normal speech of characters who are a bit odd, but not altogether insane.

To write serviceable dialogue, you need to pay attention to *how* people speak: not to turn yourself into a tape-recorder, but to observe and replicate the overall patterns of human speech, its rhythms and tones. Though occasionally you may overhear a pithy remark, a deft rejoinder, or even a thrilling exchange, when you listen you should listen not so much for content as for *style*. Keep your notebook handy. Occasionally a line or two might work its way into a story or chapter in progress. More importantly, you'll sharpen your ear for dialogue.

You'll do the same by reading great dialogue. Here's Joyce, master mimic:

> —The blessings of God on you, Buck Mulligan cried, jumping from his chair. Sit down. Pour out the tea there. The sugar is in the bag. Here, I can't go fumbling at the damned eggs. He hacked through the fry on the dish and slapped out three plates, saying:
> —*In nomine Patris et Filii et Spiritus Sancti.*
> Haines sat down to pour out tea.
> —I'm giving you two lumps each, he said. But, I say, Mulligan, you do make strong tea, don't you?
> Buck Mulligan, hewing thick slices from his loaf, said in an old woman's wheedling voice:

> —When I makes tea I makes tea, as old
> mother Grogan said. And when I makes water I
> makes water.
> —By Jove, it is tea, Haines said.
> Buck Mulligan went on hewing and whee-
> dling.
> —*So I do, Mrs. Cahill,* says she. *Begob,
> ma'am, says Mrs. Cahill, God send you don't
> make them in the one pot.*
> —James Joyce, *Ulysses*

Joyce doesn't just mimic the voices of his characters, he mimics them mimicking other voices. Here dialogue conveys not only character, but region and education, and with wit, economy, and sly playfulness. To express these qualities otherwise would have taken paragraphs or pages of inert, dry description. And no description, no matter how concisely, cleverly, or poetically rendered, reads as "wet" as dialogue. We hear people speak; we listen to the sounds of tongues moving behind and around wet lips; we prick our ears to words slick and slippery with life.

3. EXPOSITION AND DIALOGUE

Exposition conveys needed information to a reader. It does so through the narrator's own words, not through dialogue or action or dramatically, but directly through summary; not by showing but by telling.

The old saw says "show, don't tell." But there's nothing wrong with telling. It saves time and space, and helps us stick to the present action of our stories by making it unnecessary to dramatize (for instance) things that happened in the past (i.e., through flashbacks).

Of course, exposition may also carry the reader through a story's present action, summing up in a paragraph the events of a day or a week or ten years. Again, depending on the work, lest you end up with a three-thousand-page novel you may *need* such moments of summary.

The drawback to exposition is that it's less dramatic, less viscerally stimulating for the reader to read, and most readers prefer the swift pace of action and dialogue to the slow build up of exposition—especially when exposition is handled dryly, without flair, music, wit, or poetry, in what some writers call journalese. Write with a poet's sensibility and lust for language, and you can get away with reams of exposition. Or hope to.

Plot information can also be carried by dialogue, but at the risk of that dialogue seeming contrived. If you have a character say, for instance, "How's it going, Ed? Gee, it's been awhile since we seen each other, ain't it? Since that time I saw you throw that drink at Jarred Reynold's face at the fundraiser—where was it? At the White Owl Inn, wasn't it? Boy, you sure tied one on that night …" you are forcing exposition into your characters' mouths: information that the reader may need, but which subverts the quality of normal conversation. People just don't talk that way.

Better to let the characters say what they will, while interjecting, through expository narrative, whatever background is essential for the reader's comprehension of the scene. Best to do so briefly, in small bits scattered throughout the dialogue.

Chapter IV

Here's my quick fix:

> "Ed *Donovan?*" I said. "Damned if it isn't
> you! How the hell *are* you?" I walked straight up
> to him, whisky in hand. Seeing me approach he
> turned away. But I wouldn't let it go at that.
>
> "Gee, it's been a long time since we saw each
> other, hasn't it? Couple of months?" In fact I knew
> exactly how long it had been: three months and six
> days to the time I watched him throw a gin gimlet
> in Jarred Reynold's face at the White Owl Inn. But I
> had to rub his nose in it.
>
> "The Republican primary fundraiser, wasn't
> that it?" I said, rubbing away.

Dialogue can carry information, a lot of information, in fact. But when carried by dialogue, information should come in bite-sized bits. In his *Writing a Novel*, John Braine provides us with this good example of bad dialogue as a murderous cuckold bursts into a bar:

> "I'll kill that bastard, Tavers. He's taken off with my
> wife, Hilda. When I came home at six she'd gone
> and taken the kids. She left this note. The note said
> …" (etc.)

The thing to do (perhaps) is tease out the information among two or more characters, rather than force it in large chunks out of one character's mouth. Here is Braine's fix:

> "That bastard," said Tom. "I'll kill him. I swear to
> God I'll kill him." He looked as if he were going to
> vomit; his face was flushed and there were beads

of sweat around his mouth and on his forehead. I
put my hand on his arm. He was trembling vio-
lently. "Calm down. Who are you going to kill?"

Remember, the main purpose of dialogue is not to convey information, small talk, or plot points, but to evoke character and, by extension, entertain.

Here's a lovely bit of dialogue from the opening of William Kennedy's Pulitzer Prize-winning novel *Ironweed*.
Francis and his pal Rudy are stumblebum gravediggers. Francis has just returned from a solemn visit to a certain grave.

> "Whattayou been up to?" Rudy asked. "You
> know somebody buried up there?"
> "A little kid I used to know."
> "A kid? What'd he do, die young?"
> "Pretty young."
> "What happened to him?"
> "He fell."
> "He fell where?"
> "He fell on the floor."
> "Hell, I fall on the floor about twice a day
> and I ain't dead."
> "That's what you think."

The kid in question is Francis' infant son, who died when
his father dropped him by accident on the kitchen floor. All
this will eventually be made clear. Here, though, it's enough
to know that a dead boy who obviously meant something to
the protagonist lies in this grave: We read on to learn more.

What lies under that gravestone is Francis' tragic past, a past that goes far if not all the way to explaining how he has come to his present, less than dignified circumstances. Yet here tragedy is leavened with comedy by Rudy's remark about falling twice daily on his head, which in turn is met with Francis' cutting rejoinder, "That's what you think."

Kennedy's dialogue succeeds largely by virtue of its playfulness. And playfulness is the first quality of genius. When children play they reinvent the world. When writers write great dialogue, they reinvent dialogue. All the more reason to be a genius.

Such dialogue is rarely forced into characters' mouths but arises from their circumstances, to where we writers can do little more than sit back like stenographers and record, injecting a few words of exposition here and there, a gesture, a bit of action or description. Put authentic character into circumstances where their deepest needs are denied or challenged, and you can be pretty sure that they'll talk. And when they do, your job is to listen, to select and record, and then to give final shape to their words.

I hear some of you protesting, saying, "What if my characters refuse to speak? What then?" Just as, when writing exposition you listen to and hear the sound of your own voice, you "hear" those of your characters. Note the quotation marks. This is not a case of *literal* voices speaking to you as they do to schizophrenics (and perhaps to some blessed writers). When it comes to dialogue, the distinction between your own internal voice and those of your characters may be a false and therefore deceptive one, since after all they are as much a part of you as Adam's rib. *All dialogue is between the self and the soul.* When parts of your own soul speak to you through your characters, the result is good dialogue.

4. CHARACTERIZATION THROUGH DIALOGUE

> *"Dialogue is the way to nail character."*
> —Anne Lamott

We've discussed ways by which character is evoked in fiction, singling out dialogue as one of the most effective. Listen to Bartleby in Melville's "Bartleby the Scrivener":

"Bartleby," said I, "Ginger Nut is away; just step around to the post office, won't you? (It was but a three minutes walk), and see if there is anything for me."

"I would prefer not to."

"You *will* not?"

"I *prefer* not."

I staggered to my desk and sat there in a deep study. My blind inveteracy returned. Was there any other thing in which I could procure myself to be ignominiously repulsed by this lean, penniless wight?—my hired clerk? What added thing is there, perfectly reasonable, that he will be sure to refuse to do?

"Bartleby!"

No answer.

"Bartleby," in a louder tone.

No answer.

"Bartleby," I roared.

> Like a very ghost, agreeably to the laws of magical invocation, at the third summons he appeared at the entrance of his hermitage.
>
> "Go to the next room, and tell Nippers to come to me."
>
> "I prefer not to," he respectfully and slowly said, and mildly disappeared.

In four short words, "I prefer not to", we have the distilled essence of Bartleby, his perfume, if you like. He is known by those words no less than another Melville character is identified by the words "Call me Ishmael." In Ishmael's case, the words resound like sledgehammer blows, while Bartleby's refrain is played on something more like a xylophone.

But even one line of dialogue can strike a definitive blow in defining a character. Take Father Egan, the drunken priest in Robert Stone's novel *A Flag for Sunrise.* After the murderous Lieutenant Campos has tried to shoot him (only to find his service revolver empty), Campos turns to Father Egan apologetically and says, "I have no more cartridges."

Father Egan replies: "Well, I haven't any."

Could any of us have come up with a more perfect line?

Remember, it's not what characters should or would say that counts; it's what they *do* say, prompted by their own (meaning your) deepest instincts. *All dialogue is between the self and the soul.* The self is you, the soul is your characters. Cast them in situations wherein they must speak, and they *will* speak. All you have to do is listen.

5. DIALOGUE & PACING

Because dialogue reads faster than any other part of fiction, it plays a big role in setting the pace of our stories or novels. Think of yourself as driving a car called fiction. When writing a descriptive passage, you're easing off the gas and stepping on the brake pedal. Introduce dialogue, and you're stepping on the gas again. The story careens forward.

Compare:

> … She was modest about words, particularly big ones, therefore it seemed all the more powerful when she herself suddenly embraced me from behind and whispered that she loved me. Once I asked her why, but she just smiled and said because. Because what? She looked at me as if she was surprised I could bring myself to ask. Because you're so stupid, she replied and kissed me on the brow. To her there was no why or wherefore, and there was almost a touch of disappointment in her smile, as if I had come to reveal that I was not as sure as she was. But as reticent as she was towards words, toward the belief that everything can be explained, and as cool and reserved as she could seem to those around us when we were out, she found it equally easy to let herself go when we were alone together.

to:

> Terry continued to stare at the yard that sloped down to the road, the clay hardpack turned dark

in the rain.

"And we kill some more where we have the roadblock and stop all the drivers and look at the identity cards. The ones we want we take in the bush and kill them."

The man paused and Terry waited. The guy wasn't confessing his sins, he was bragging about what he did.

"You hear me, Fatha?"

Terry said, "Keep talking," wondering where the guy was going with it.

Unlike Europeans, we Americans (who love fast cars, fast food, anything fast) favor lots of dialogue in fiction. Though a bestseller in its native Denmark—and gorgeously written—a book like Jens Christian Grondahl's *Silence in October* (from which the first of the above two paragraphs is drawn) was a hard sell for audiences here, consisting as it does of page after page of dense expository prose, with some paragraphs several pages long, and not a word of direct dialogue. Other good (or bad, depending how you look at it) examples of works with little dialogue are those of Samuel Beckett, whose sublimely boring novels abstain not only from dialogue but from anything more dramatic or kinetic than a man moving a series of stones from various pockets to his mouth.

Most of our countrymen prefer Raymond Carver or Hemingway, whose stories are chockablock with dialogue, or someone like Elmore Leonard, author of the second passage (from *Pagan Babies),* who freely admits that he hates describing things and boasts that when writing he skips the parts that most readers skip: meaning just about everything but the dialogue.

Good for Elmore Leonard. And good for you, if you want to write like him. As I've said, readers seldom tire of dialogue, which may make you wonder how you can have too much of a good thing. On the other hand we're artists, not deli workers making sandwiches to order. We have to write what moves us, and every story seeks its own perfect form, whether that form is aggressively commercial or not.

Personally, I'll read a book with little or no dialogue. But that book had better be a work of art. Otherwise I'd as soon read Elmore Leonard.

6. Contractions and Phonetic Spellings

Unless inflamed by emotion ("I—will—not!"), people tend to speak in contractions. And so should your characters. A character who says, "I do not understand what it is that you are doing," sounds stilted and Spock-like. Unless he's a Vulcan, you'll want to throw in some contractions ("I don't see what you're doing").

Contractions have their place not only in dialogue, but in narration, to give a more natural or casual flow to a sentence, or simply to adjust its rhythm. Even a writer as formally elegant as Virginia Woolf feels compelled, occasionally, to resort to them: "There wasn't the slightest possible chance that they could go to the Lighthouse tomorrow." In cases like this, your ear is the best judge—another argument for reading your work out loud.

When writing in first person you also have to take into

[117]

account the diction of your narrator. There would be something odd indeed about a Huck Finn who said, "You would not know about me unless you have read a book entitled, *The Adventures of Tom Sawyer*, by Mr. Mark Twain." Without contractions, Huck ain't Huck.

But then some authors take this notion to extremes through the use—or abuse—of phonetic spellings, spellings that duplicate a character's peculiar dialect and/or pronunciation. An extreme example:

> Aw, ah sais. Ah wanted the radge tae jist fuck off ootay ma visage, tae go oan his ain, n jist leave us wi Jean-Claude. Oan the other hand, ah'd be gitting sick tae before long. … They call um Sick Boy, no because he's eywis sick wi junk withdrawal, but because he's one sick—
> —Irvine Welsh, *Trainspotting*

At first glance this looks daunting, if not completely impossible. Yet with some effort you can make sense of it. The trick is to read out loud. Do this with the above passage and you'll find yourself transformed into a lower class Edinburgh youth who spends his days watching, through a heroin-induced miasma, freight trains rolling over the Scottish countryside.

Worth the effort? Since the book has been a huge critical and commercial success (and has been made into an equally successful film), the short answer has to be yes. But that doesn't mean you or I will necessarily consider it worth it. And you can be sure that for every game reader who slogged his way through this peat bog of *daes* and *aws*, three others clambered to firmer ground, and will never know what a blue-nosed Weegie gadgie is (an underprivileged member of the Glasgow Protestant community.)

So such novelty acts can be performed, but at the risk of alienating your audience. A safer tact is to spell words normally and let the choice and arrangement of words, or their syntax, convey dialect or accent.

Here's a dialogue sample from a story of my own, "To Die of Italy," set in northern Italy, in which, by implication, the uncle character speaks Italian:

> Throughout the meal, even with his mouth full, Uncle Sergio never stopped talking except to suck his teeth.
>
> "How is your mother, my darling, beautiful sister! The flower of my heart! When I am alone, I think of her and I am happy! I have thousands of photographs—all of my sister and my *nipote* and your father, my American family! And the dog! What is the dog's name? Pal! How is my little Pal?"
>
> "Pal is dead," I murmured.
>
> "What a shame. Such a lovely dog—it makes me cry! Come closer: why do you sit so far away, you mischievous devil, you bandit, you! Give your uncle a kiss!"
>
> He thrust his big wet face at me; I drew back.
>
> "You are right, *nipote,* you are much too big for that sort of thing now. What muscles you have, for the love of God! May I squeeze them? Oh, I forgot: you don't like to be touched. My *nipote*— the Greek god! Do you know about the Greeks?"

CHAPTER **IV**

The sense of a foreign tongue being spoken is conveyed by the stiff, formal and faintly archaic syntax, which has the quality of a literal and thus a not-very-good translation of the words being spoken. The reader may or may not grasp this. Still, he gets it without having to be told that, by the way, the character is speaking Italian. Not only does such a method avoid insulting the reader's intelligence, it involves him more deeply in the scene by assuming a certain familiarity and sophistication, while suggesting that author and reader are in cahoots, collaborators.

A good writer can also avoid mechanical or clumsy dialogue by simply telling the reader how things are said. Instead of having Carlos say, "I d-d-d-d-d-d-don't know," simply append the words, "Carlos said, stammering," to his dialogue. If nothing else you'll save wear on your keyboard.

7. STAGE DIRECTIONS AND GESTURES

With dialogue, it's best to let your characters' voices do as much of the work as possible, while trying not to intrude. It's not necessary, for instance, to describe every action or gesture of your speakers. One or two telling gestures will do.

You might mention, for instance, that when sitting and talking Boris has the unpleasant habit of jiggling his right leg up and down, while his chain-smoking wife, Irene, twirls a strand of gray hair behind her ear with nicotine-stained fingers.

Otherwise, stay out of it. Unless it really tells us something about a character, don't record banal gestures. "She took a breath and exhaled," tells me nothing about a character other than that her respiratory system is functioning. Because they serve no purpose, such stage directions are intrusive. When characters speak, readers mainly want to listen, and unless it adds something, the narrator's voice is Brian Epstein getting on stage with the Beatles.

This is especially true when the dialogue is emotionally charged. Here, in this example from Chekhov's "A Trifle From Life," a man tries to extract from the child of his mistress information about her husband:

> "… Does [your] father say anything about me?"
> "Like what?"
> "Anything."
> "Nothing special." Alyosha shrugged.
> "What did he say?"
> "You sure you won't get mad?"
> "Why? What did he say?"
> "He says mother's unhappy because of you. That it's your fault that she's ruined. But don't listen to him. You know how weird he gets. I said you were nice, that you never yell at her or anything like that, but he just shook his head."

Dialogue here carries the whole scene. Knowing this, except to mention that one shrug, the narrator doesn't interrupt; he tells us nothing but what we need to know, and what we need to know is what is *said*.

In his effort to "butt out" Chekhov even keeps his attributions to a minimum. Attributions are the little tag lines that tell us who has just spoken or is speaking, and may also indicate how something is said, often redundantly.

"I hate your miserable guts!" she blurted bitterly.

Not only is the alliteration unwelcome, both the bitterness and the blurting are implied by the line itself. Never state what's implied.

When well written, most dialogue tells us how it should be read. Take any play by Shakespeare, divide up the dialogue, present each actor with only his or her lines and cues (sides, these are called), have them enter and speak and behold—the words are so deftly chosen and arranged that they direct themselves, with rhythms and accents falling precisely where needed to force inflection and convey the proper tones.

You don't have to be Shakespeare to trust your readers. We usually know when a character feels angry, or is being ironic, or playful. What interests readers isn't how a line of dialogue is spoken; that they can usually figure out.

But they may be interested in the facial expression or a telling gesture that may accompany what is said. In such cases the gesture or expression isn't arbitrary or banal, but revealing—or what poker players call a *tell*. When Hank scratches his nose, we know he's lying. When Sheila casts a watery glance across the banquet hall at her husband, we know she's about to cheat on him again. Such gestures augment or even take the place of dialogue.

8. SAID AND OTHER ATTRIBUTIVE VERBS

Usually, we writers want our words to carry weight, to be—as I said before—as hefty as stones, to have an impact. But there is at least one exception.

Said—that most weightless and watery of words—is the perfect host to dialogue: smooth, discreet, all but invisible, like the butler in Kazuo Ishiguro's *Remains of the Day*. Stop killing yourself to come up with new, improved ways of saying *he said*. No need for *chuckled, barked, sighed, groaned*. No need to have your characters *intone, utter* or (heaven forbid) *opine* things, or *spit, blurt, laugh,* or *bark* them. Nor is there cause to have them *affirm* something with (or without) *conviction,* when they could just as easily say "Yes." Or better still, nod.

I don't mean to imply that *said* is the only allowable attributive. In all 340 pages of Nelson Algren's delectably oddball *The Man with the Golden Arm,* no character ever "says" anything. Rather, they *agreed / wanted to know / pointed out / assured / replied / demanded / told him / warned / called / mourned / decided / put in cunningly.* Algren is a master at avoiding *said.* On the other hand Robert Stone, no less fine an author, never uses any other attribution.

Both are brave, honorable men.

You have to find your own way, follow your own rules. But whatever rules you set for yourself should be based on the demands of your material coupled with a cast-iron aesthetic, and not on fashion, or the desperate ploys of an attention-starved ego.

9. SOME LAST WORDS ON DIALOGUE

Once you get good at it, writing dialogue should be a pleasure. It's like coasting on a bicycle, only the characters do all the work, not gravity. Your biggest worry then is making sure your characters don't run off at the mouth and talk your story to death. Like cattle, they need to be nudged along and allowed to range only so far before being herded back into the corral.

Here are a few more words of advice regarding dialogue:

Make it concise. The fewer words to make a point, the better. Having transcribed the speech from your characters lips, go back and cut, cut, cut—to the bone—keeping only those lines that convey character and thus entertain.

Consider the subtext. What people say and what they really mean are often different things, with meaning often buried *under* the lines, and not floating on them. This is especially true of theatrical dialogue, where subtext gives the actors something to play. In Marsha Norman's Pulitzer Prize-winning drama, *'Night Mother,* about a young woman's decision to commit suicide and her mother's vain efforts to stop her, when the girl asks her mother, "Do we have any old towels?" the unspoken subtext of that line is, "I'm going to blow my brains out in the bathroom and don't want to make a big mess."

Be illogical. People are, especially when they speak—especially when they argue. For this reason dialogue shouldn't always make sense. Nor do people listen when they speak; even if they do, they often don't respond directly to what's just been said. When writing dialogue, try, every three or four lines at least, to "deal from the bottom of the deck," to have characters say something surprising if not bizarre, or at least not obvious.

"Tell me about it."

"Humph."

"Eat me."

"Huh? What's that?"

"I said tell me about it. Explain about the Japanese to a guy who doesn't know."

"You know what *uni* is?"

"Forgive my ignorance."

"That's the national food of Japan, son. That's the whole story around Muscunguspoint anymore, unless you count the Scientologists camped out in that damn hotel. Japanese family's got to eat *uni* least once a week to maintain their self-respect. Like you'd want a steak, they want a plate of urchin eggs."

In the above-quoted passage from Jonathan Lethem's *Motherless Brooklyn*, the character who says "eat me" has Tourette's syndrome, and so neither he nor his creator can be held totally responsible for his outbursts. But to utter fresh dialogue your characters needn't be so afflicted. The simple truth being that, like Art Linkletter's kids, we all say the darndest things.

Be adversarial. The essence of most strong dialogue can be distilled to the following two-word exchange:

"Please—"

"No."

We learn more when characters quarrel, when their philosophies, desires and feelings clash. As Dostoevsky did, let your characters spill their opinionated guts all over the page. Then go back, cut and trim (or end up with a cinder-block-sized, nineteenth-century Russian novel).

Entertain. Above all, dialogue should amuse. It amuses because it comes from the souls of unique characters with strong personalities. A character whose every utterance is flat, predictable, or a cliché is a dull character.

Scene: a training class for taxi drivers, forty or fifty men sitting in rows of little desks bolted to the floor. Roll is taken. The lesson begins:

> "Now most guys think they know how to drive. But the fact is very few people know how to drive, they just steer. Every time I drive down the street I marvel at the fact that there isn't an accident every few seconds. Every day I see two or three people simply run through red lights as if they didn't exist. I'm no preacher but I can tell you this—the lives that people live are driving them crazy and their insanity comes out in the way they drive. I'm not here to tell you how to live. You'll have to see your rabbi or your priest or your local whore. I'm here to teach you how to drive. I'm trying to keep our insurance rates down, and to fix it so you can get back to your room alive at night."
>
> "God damn," said the kid next to me, "old Smithson's something, ain't he?"
>
> "Every man is a poet," I said.
>
> "Now," said Smithson, "and, god damn you, McBride, wake up and listen to me … now, when is the only time a man can lose control of his cab and won't be able to help it?"
>
> "When I get a hard-on?" said some cracker.

"Mendoza, if you can't drive with a hard-on we can't use you. Some of our best men drive with hard-ons all day long and all night too."

The boys laughed.

"Come on, when is the only time a man can lose control of his cab and won't be able to help it?" Nobody answered. I raised my hand.

"Yes, Chinaski?"

"A man might lose control of his cab when he sneezed."

"That's correct."

I felt like a star pupil again. It was like the old L.A. City College days—bad grades, but good with the mouth.

—Charles Bukowski, *Factotum*

Hearing my characters' voices welling up inside me, I dive in, pen, pencil, or computer at hand, and meet them halfway.

You do the same.

CHAPTER V:
Description

"… to make you hear, to make you feel;
but above all to make you see."
—*Joseph Conrad*

V. DESCRIPTION

Whether summary or scene, all writing is descriptive. But if writing good dialogue demands that you slip quietly into the wings and let your characters take center stage, description is your big chance to steal the limelight and chew up some scenery, while pitching your voice to the chandeliers. Think of Maria Callas belting an aria in *Tosca*, or Charlie Parker climbing a brass ladder to the moon. Description gives wings to your authorial voice and lets it soar.

> Morning began dull and numb, then brightened miraculously. I tramped the neighborhood. It was warm and earnest at one o'clock, with a tide of summer odors from the stockyards and the sewers (odors so old in the city-bred memory they are no longer repugnant).
>
> In the upper light there were small fair heads of cloud turning. The streets, in contrast, looked burnt-out; the chimneys pointed heavenward in openmouthed exhaustion. The turf, intersected by sidewalk, was bedraggled with the whole winter's deposit of deadwood, match cards, cigarettes,

> dogmire, rubble.
> The grass behind the palings and wrought-iron
> frills was still yellow, although in many places
> the sun had already succeeded in shaking it into
> livelier green. And the houses, their doors and
> windows open, drawing in the freshness, were like
> old drunkards or consumptives taking a cure.
> —Saul Bellow, *Dangling Man*

Topping the long list of Saul Bellow's prodigious gifts was his ability to describe the American landscape, especially its cities, as in the above example from his second novel, *Dangling Man*. The settings of Bellow's novels are as human as his characters; the buildings and houses breathe, suffer and spawn; city buses poison pedestrians with their fumes. Bellow not only captures the sensation of things, but "the sensation," V.S. Prichett writes in *The Tale Bearers*, "that the things have created [Bellow's] people or permeated them." Such descriptive prowess does more than set or dress the stage: it floods it with character and drama; it chews up the very scenery it creates.

Every description need not be a show-stopper. Though descriptions provide us with opportunities to air our authorial lungs, there are humbler reasons for describing things.

1. TO EXPLAIN THE UNFAMILIAR

Whether your story takes place at the dawn of the Chinese Revolution or in a backroom poker parlor, unless you familiarize readers with your milieu they may fail to grasp the subtle twists in your plot. You needn't roll out the map of

Shanghai, quote Chairman Mao, or recite long passages of Slansky's *Theory of Poker*. But some description is called for to orient readers to what might otherwise be a completely alien landscape, and give them solid ground to stand on.

Ever mainline heroin? Read Nelson Algren's *The Man With the Golden Arm* and you'll feel as if you have:

> It hit all right. It hit the heart like a runaway loco-
> motive, it hit like a falling wall. Frankie's whole
> body lifted with that smashing surge, the very heart
> seemed to lift up-up-up—then rolled over and
> he slipped into a long warm bath with one long
> orgasmic sigh of relief. Frankie opened his eyes. …
> He was in a room. Somebody's dust-colored wavy-
> walled room and he wasn't quite dead after all.

When Algren wrote this passage he'd never tried hero-in; he had an aversion to needles. Yet he knew addicts and trusted his knowledge and imagination to get it right. Algren throws not just his fancy but his whole body into this passage, becoming Frankie "Machine" Majcinek as the "hit" blasts through his blood "like a runaway locomotive." Note the doubling-up of similes, with Algren squirming for the right image as his protagonist squirms under the needle, and those up-up-ups clawing their way out of agony.

To the novelist nothing human is alien. Not even mur-der. Here's how, in *Man's Fate*, André Malraux describes that act:

> The sleeper, lying on his back in his European-style
> bed, was wearing only a pair of short drawers,

> but his ribs were not visible under the full flesh. Ch'en had to take the nipples as gauging points. He tried holding the dagger with the blade up. But the left breast was the one away from him: he would have to strike at arm's length through the mosquito-netting. He changed the position of the dagger: blade down. To touch this motionless body was as difficult as to stab a corpse, perhaps for the same reason.

Note the attention paid here to specific details, which, in any other context, might seem banal. That the sleeper's bed is European-style; that he sleeps in short drawers, that his full flesh hides his ribs: Who cares about such things? The murderer does, and so do we, since through those details we enter his mind.

To describe the unfamiliar requires that you familiarize yourself with your subject, and if you haven't done so already, that means doing some research. With this cautionary note: nothing helps writers procrastinate more than doing research and taking notes. I was once told of a (perhaps apocryphal) writer who spent twenty-five years researching a novel, piling up page after page of notes, until the pages practically drove him out of his home. Sadly, the poor man died before he could actually get down to writing his book. Then again, had he lived, he'd probably have gone on with his "research."

Okay, so you don't believe it either. But it makes a good point. Research just enough to feel competent at discussing your subject. You don't need to be a brain surgeon to discuss brain surgery or to *sound like* a brain surgeon. If, on the other hand, you find yourself itching to drill through people's skulls and get at their frontal lobes, odds are you've done too much research.

2. TO BREATHE LIFE INTO THE FAMILIAR

Your descriptive arsenal shouldn't only be aimed at things exotic. Now and then you need to make the familiar fresh, to rouse the jaded reader who sits with arms smugly folded thinking, "Been there; done that." For such readers description may be your only salvation.

Take New York City on a hot summer day. Been there? Done *that?* I figured as much. But have you been to this particular New York during this specific summer:

> It was a queer, sultry summer, the summer they electrocuted the Rosenbergs, and I didn't know what I was doing in New York. I'm stupid about executions. The idea of being electrocuted makes me sick, and that's all there was to read about in the papers—goggle-eyed headlines staring up at me on every street corner and at the fusty, peanut-smelling mouth of every subway. It had nothing to do with me, but I couldn't help wondering what it would be like, being burned alive all along your nerves.
> —Sylvia Plath, *The Bell Jar*

Having written her first and only novel, poet Sylvia Plath saw it rejected thrice in her own country before publishing it in England under the pseudonym Victoria Lucas (she had decided by then that it was not a "serious work").

She wrote it to make a grab at the wider audience that shuns poets and poetry.

Yet in this opening paragraph the serious poet is alive and well. Plath may have been stupid about electrocutions, but when it came to describing things she was no dummy. Take those "goggle-eyed" headlines. Who but a major poet puts goggles on a newspaper to strike a vivid, dead-on image? As for that "fusty, peanut-smelling" subway, I've lived in New York City now for over thirty years and have yet to smell peanuts in a subway station. Yet Plath's nose for convincing detail is so sharp I can no longer ride the subway without *imagining* that smell.

I'm reminded of Picasso's famous portrait of Gertrude Stein, the one that hangs in the Metropolitan. When he painted it Stein complained, "It doesn't look like me." To which the wily Spaniard replied, "Don't worry; it will."

When describing familiar things, don't ignore the obvious ("the subway entrance was stuffy and hot") but render it in fresh terms ("fusty, peanut-smelling"). Even something as simple and familiar as a handshake can be brought to life by description. Is the man's grip "warm and friendly" or "limp as a Cantonese noodle" or "clammy like last night's chowder"? Feel it first, then describe.

3. TO CONVINCE THROUGH AUTHENTIC DETAIL

To make people believe in things that never happened, to get them to swallow your "lies": that's your job. Factual or not, some details are so startlingly specific they convince the reader that the storyteller has lived through whatever experience is put forth. When in his novel *Deliverance* (about men encountering savagery on a canoe trip in Appalachia) James Dickey describes an underwater log covered with chicken feathers as "a vague choked whiteness … with all the feather-hairs weaving and wavering in a perfect physical representation of nausea," the detail is too specific and strong to resist, and any lingering doubts as to the author's credibility and authority are put to bed.

On the other hand when a lack of authentic detail leaves room for doubt, what rushes in to fill the vacuum? Cliché. Take the following familiar scene: a fireman rushing into a burning building to rescue a baby. Forget flames: the real danger here is triteness. The reader knows just what to expect, or thinks she does. Meet those expectations perfectly and the scene fails.

So what does the brave author do? Just as the scene is about to burst into bathos, he has his fireman hear an odd, trickling sound—water hissing through pipes—that turns out to be the wax melting in his ears. As surely as fireman rescues baby his creator rescues the reader from cliché.

4. TO DEEPEN CHARACTER AND EVOKE EMOTION

Unlike clichés, good descriptions never occur in a vacuum; they are subject to the moods and emotions of the characters whose worlds they describe. A Ferris wheel slowly turning from the point of view of a little girl who has just won her first stuffed panda will differ significantly from the same Ferris wheel viewed by a man whose son has just died in the muddy trenches of World War I.

Here, in one of literature's most celebrated descriptive passages, a snowstorm seen through the eyes of a man who has just learned that his wife still holds a candle for a lover long dead:

> A few light taps upon the pane made him turn to the window. It had begun to snow again. He watched sleepily the flakes, silver and dark, falling obliquely against the lamplight … Yes, the newspapers were right: snow was general all over Ireland. It was falling on every part of the dark central plain, on the treeless hills, falling softly upon the Bog of Allen and, farther westward, softly falling into the dark mutinous Shannon waves. It was falling, too, upon every part of the lonely churchyard on the hill where Michael Fury lay buried. It lay thickly drifted on the crooked crosses and headstones, on the spears of the little gate, on the barren thorns.

For those who've never read James Joyce's "The Dead," I'll leave off the last line of this swooning aria. Some argue that Joyce goes too far, that the snow "falling softly" while also "softly falling" (and falling in a half dozen other ways) takes too many repetitive, onomatopoeic, and alliterative liberties; that the passage is gaudy. Call me a sucker for Weltschmerz; I say it's gorgeous. The repetitions are meant to lull us—like a hypnotist's watch—into a trance similar to that induced in the main character by the spectacle of the falling snow, and damned if they don't. Meanwhile, the "dark central plain," the "treeless hills," the "Bog of Allen," all point to specific places even as they stretch endlessly outward to include the universe.

But Joyce, a master of what T. S. Eliot called the *objective correlative*—things standing for feelings—could milk as much emotional significance out of the "cold white grease" deposited by a hunk of cabbage on a plate as from a cosmic midnight snowstorm.

Think of those shots in movies where the camera lingers on a broken windowpane or some such detail of setting, or does a slow sweep of somebody's dresser top, showing us the cufflinks a character wears, the brand of cigarettes he smokes, a box of wooden matches, and how he treats loose change. There are authenticating details.

Consider lingering on such details yourself, if only for a sentence or two.

5. Go in Fear of Abstractions

So—assuming that our descriptions serve a purpose, that they're properly motivated—how do we go about making them vivid?

First, by taking Ezra Pound's advice and going "in fear of abstractions." Ezra, as you probably know, went nuts. Still, when it came to advice for writers the poet who discovered Eliot and Joyce knew his elbow from third base.

When it comes to description, concrete and specific always trump abstract and general. "Sally had beautiful, strawberry-blonde hair" says little compared with "Sally's hair gleamed and tumbled, like copper turnings from a spinning lathe." The image evoked by copper turnings is concrete and specific, whereas "beautiful strawberry blonde" evokes only the vaguest notion, one sure to differ from reader to reader as one remembers Beverly Butterworth, his moon-faced second grade sweetheart, and another pictures Ann Margaret in *Carnal Knowledge.*

Abstractions have a deadening effect, appealing not to the senses but only to the intellect. And as Tolstoy tells us the purpose of fiction is to transmit *feelings*. Here's Hemingway on abstractions in *A Farewell to Arms*:

> I was always embarrassed by the words sacred, glorious, and sacrifice, and the expression in vain. We had heard them, sometimes standing in the rain almost out of earshot, so that only the shouted words came through, and read them, on proclamations that were slapped up by billposters … and I had seen nothing sacred, and the things that were called glorious had no glory and the sacrifices were like the stockyards at Chicago.

Note how with one solid simile, "like the stockyards of Chicago," Papa shoots all those glorious abstractions like clay ducks out of the sky.

Long before Hemingway declared war against abstractions, Shakespeare had loaded his quill pen. Here's Wild Bill writing up a storm in *King Lear:*

> Blow, winds, and crack your cheeks! rage! Blow!
> You cataracts and hurricanes spout
> Till you have drench'd our steeples, drown'd the
>   cocks!

You sulphurous and thought-executing fires
Vaunt couriers of oak-cleaving thunderbolts,
Singe my white head! And thou, all-shaking
    thunder,
Strike flat the thick rotundity o' the world!
Crack nature's moulds, all germens spill at once,
That make ingrateful man!
Rumble thy bellyful! Spit fire! Spout rain!

Note the heavy emphasis on nouns (twenty out of sixty-seven words) and verbs (fifteen). "The great strength of our language," according to Sinologist and poet Ernest Fenollosa, "lies in its splendid array of transitive verbs." Verbs are to language what seeds and nuts are to nature: they store and release energy.

When Shakespeare does use modifiers (adjectives and adverbs), he favors temporary compounds—"thought-executing," "oak-cleaving"—noun-verb pairs that have been pressed into service as adjectives. Lear's entire storm speech holds but one pure abstraction: "ingrateful." Even the Bard nods, occasionally. Still, you have to admit, it beats the heck out of "it was a dark and stormy night."[1]

Remember, too, that though we are taught that adjectives are descriptive, they are really *judgments* about the way things look, feel, sound, taste, etc: prejudices rendered as verdicts. And (according to poet Liz Socolow) "when you

1 That infamous line, by the way, opens the novel *Paul Clifford* by Edward George-Lytton. The full passage reads: "It was a dark and stormy night; the rain fell in torrents—except at occasional intervals, when it was checked by a violent gust of wind which swept up the streets (for it is in London that our scene lies), rattling along the housetops, and fiercely agitating the scanty flame of the lamps that struggled against the darkness." As you see, modifier-wise things don't get any better.

[139]

prejudge an experience (or a reaction) you deny the reader his or her own experience, forcing him to think your way and shutting out his own reaction."

Most modifiers are filler, cotton batting or sawdust, their modifications perfunctory or already implied. When describing a crowded, noisy subway, don't lean on those lazy, obvious modifiers. Show me the red leather laces on the brogan of the construction worker who has just stepped on your protagonist's shoe; let me smell the dusky half-moon of sweat hanging from that armpit thrust into his face; let me hear the squeals of tortured steel on twisted track; let me see the tiled walls rushing by in a muddy blur. A generic subway ride most of us can live without. But a specific one may be worth at least the price of a Metrocard.

As for adverbs, they seldom add anything to an adjective that isn't already there and tend to come pre-packaged like McDonald's Happy Meals. *Raving beauty, distinct possibility, stark naked, stinking drunk* ... these are pairings so familiar they wave the red flag of cliché.

Not that you should avoid all modifiers. In skilled hands adverbs and adjectives truly spice up the nouns and verbs they touch. In his black comedy epic, *Catch-22*, when Joseph Heller (who adores his modifiers) describes General Dreedle's "ruddy, monolithic" face he adds something to that face that wouldn't be there otherwise. When he endows obsequious military men with "efficient mouths and inefficient eyes," the reader believes she knows exactly what he means, though she has no idea.

Likewise when Jorge Luis Borges writes in *The Circular Ruins*, "No one saw him disembark in the unanimous night," only a dunce editor would take a red pencil to that adjective. "Go in fear of abstractions" doesn't mean never use them: it means use them boldly, bravely—but sparingly, as a chef uses cilantro.

Go through your descriptions, hunt down the abstractions, see if you can't firm them up with solid things. A fellow author recently described a kitchen in the aftermath of a broken affair as "smelling of sorrow." I challenged her to tell me what sorrow smells like. She thought for a moment and answered, "Burnt toast." And into the description it went.

6. Simile / Metaphor

The shortest route to description is by way of comparison. A simile is a stated comparison, a metaphor an implied one. "Wesley's mouth is an open sewer" is—we hope—a metaphor. Add like and you get a simile.

My (breakable) rule being this: If you can change a simile into a metaphor without confusing us, do it. Why say what something's *like* when you can say what it *is?* In *Miss Lonelyhearts,* his novel about an advice columnist, Nathaniel West, having originally written "and on most days I received more than thirty letters, all of them alike, as though stamped from the dough of suffering with a heart-shaped cookie knife," cut the words "as though," changing a strong simile into a stronger metaphor. The lesson: never state what you can imply.

Whatever figurative device you use, the result should relate to your fictional world. If your story is set in the North Pole and you want to compare Howard to a bear, make him a Polar bear. If your setting is Wall Street, make him a Brinks truck.

Lousy at metaphor? Don't despair. There's a metaphor muscle: the more we use it, the stronger it gets. It helps, too, to study the masters:

> He looked up at me from underneath a tattered revolution of old blankets.
> —Richard Brautigan, *Trout Fishing in America*

> I felt as though I was carrying that cadaver's head around with me on a string, like some black, noseless balloon stinking of vinegar.
> —Sylvia Plath, *The Bell Jar*

> His hair is made of straw. His ideas are straw. His wife too is straw, though still a little damp.
> —Henry Miller, *Tropic of Cancer*

> The Mother knows her own face is a big white dumpling of worry.
> —Lorrie Moore, *Birds of America*

About mixing metaphors: don't. If the stage floor under the spotlights looks like a stretch of sandy beach, the shifting, murmuring audience might be likened to surf, but not to a windblown field of Kansas corn.

7. SETTING AND THE SENSES

Plot and suspense may quicken our pulses, and ideas engage the intellect, but description arouses the senses: sight, smell, sound, touch, taste. Over the thin outline of story the prose artist paints in thick impasto strokes, adding flesh to bare bone, turning airy ideas into solid matter.

This holds true especially in descriptions of settings. However dramatic, action and dialogue don't take place in a void. Setting supplies the time and space dimensions of a scene, the when and where. Think of your characters as actors and the setting as the stage on which they perform.

In some stories, setting plays its own dramatic role. Think of Jack London's "To Build a Fire" in which a prospector, struggling to survive through a night in the frozen Klondike, must build a fire or freeze to death; or Stephen Crane's "The Open Boat," about four shipwreck survivors in a lifeboat, with its memorable first line, "None of them knew the color of the sky."

It's hard to name any novel or story in which setting doesn't play a crucial, if not a fateful, role. Set *Madame Bovary*, the story of an adulterous affair and its tragic consequences, in present day Beverly Hills, and watch it evaporate. *Dr. Zhivago* in the tropics? Impossible.

In Marilynne Robinson's novel *Housekeeping*, the floodwaters of Fingerbone Lake lap at every scene:

> It is true that one is always aware of the lake in Fingerbone, or the deeps of the lake, the lightless, airless waters below. When the ground is plowed in the spring, cut and laid open, what exhales from the furrows but that same, sharp, watery smell. The wind is watery, and all the pumps and creeks and ditches smell of water unalloyed by any other element. At the foundation is the old lake, which is smothered and nameless and alto-

gether black. ...
—Marilynne Robinson, *Housekeeping*

Robinson's setting is so well evoked, her world so persuasively sodden, when not dripping the pages reek of mildew. Note how she renders water not visually, as most of us would, but through the nose, in terms of its smell: that most powerful sense and so underutilized by writers.

Descriptions are most effective when they engage more than one sensory organ. Here's a passage from one of my own stories, "Deus ex Machina," wherein a small-town boy rides in his city-slicker uncle's convertible:

> We followed my dad's white Pinto out into traffic. I saw puffs of blue smoke coming out of his rusty tailpipe, and the back of his balding head jerking back and forth when he shifted. Even though we were going exactly the same speed, with the top down and the wind whipping my hair, the Karmann Ghia felt twice as fast as my father's car. The smell of my uncle's aftershave mixed with the smell of damp air and exhaust fumes.

By including the senses of touch and smell, the scene gains in dimension and the reader feels more thoroughly grounded in the moment. Real life is experienced through all the senses: why should fiction be otherwise?

But settings need not be sensuous to be evocative. Remember Hemingway's "The Killers," quoted earlier in the section on point of view? That description works wonders at evoking setting and mood, with its two cold-blooded killers in their derby hats starkly silhouetted against a bare-bones

[144]

set rendered in flat sentences. A spark of poetry would ignite that cardboard and plywood set and send it up in flames. Its lack of poetry makes it poetic.

8. SELECTIVITY: THE QUICK & THE DEAD

Still, our descriptions can't be too inclusive; we have to make choices. And not just to save paper, but because good descriptions involve the reader: they're collaborative, a meeting of minds between writer and audience. To paint every leaf of the tree is to flatten the viewer's experience of that tree, to lock her out of it. The best descriptions tend to be impressionistic, seizing on a few select details, while letting the reader—whose imagination wields a swifter, more skillful brush than Vermeer—do the rest.

But how to make that selection? How to choose between what D. H. Lawrence called "the quick and the dead"?

Trust your instincts. When you see someone walking toward you down a hospital corridor, what are the first things you notice? Those are the things to describe. The smells of carbolic acid and iodine; the squish of disposable slippers on spinach-colored linoleum. Sometimes a line or two does the trick:

> The [hotel] clerk had been working over the chicken, cracking the bones and sucking the marrow. Her hair was thin and her teeth were leaning gray ruins in her lipless mouth.
> —Charles D'Ambrosio, "The Dead Fish Museum"

[145]

While some descriptions K.O. us like a one-two punch, others tend to linger, slowing the action to a crawl or stopping it completely. In his novel, *The Corrections*, Jonathan Franzen favors the lingering approach:

> … the random Nordstrum shopping bag that was camped behind the dust ruffle … would contain the whole shuffled pathos of a refugee existence —non-consecutive issues of Good Housekeeping, black-and-white snapshots of Enid in the 1940s, brown recipes on high-acid paper that called for wilted lettuce, the current month's telephone and gas bills, the detailed First Notice from the medical lab instructing co-payers to ignore subsequent billings for less than fifty cents.

Like the march of boxcars clacking over the tracks as we wait for the freight train to pass, lists have a built-in music to them. The contents of a medicine cabinet or a trunk can tell us more about a character than eight pages of psychobabble. In the example above (of which I've quoted a mere sliver), the mother whose attic we are excavating—and to whom these precious worthless items belong—is, by proxy, precisely and lovingly rendered. What makes this a moving portrait and not a laundry list is the level of specific detail. Had Franzen simply written "a bunch of old recipes," we'd peg mom a stereotype and feed his novel to the paper shredder. But they're not just any old recipes, they're "recipes on high-acid paper that called for wilted lettuce." Franzen doesn't just specify, he specifies the specification. As with cliché, at that level of detail stereotype doesn't stand a chance.

But even when listing particulars, discretion must be exercised. An exhaustive catalogue might interest the historian or the archeologist, but in readers it's more likely to induce catatonia. It's up to us to balance specificity with concision, detail with discretion.

9. AVOID INERT DESCRIPTION

Cut off from character and action, our descriptions read like items in a glass museum display case, curious but inert. If I write, "A warm breeze blew through the open window," that breeze blows strictly for itself and effects nothing. If I write, "The breeze through the open window warmed Maggie's skin and made her think of summers on Martha's Vineyard," I'm not just shooting the breeze but describing something that's happening to someone. And since fiction has but one subject, and that subject is people, no description should exist separate and apart from that subject.

Here's a description I labored on for some time, of a trip on the Staten Island Ferry at dusk. My first go:

> By the time the ferry leaves it is late afternoon;
> the sun is setting. Seagulls wheel over the gar-
> bage-strewn waves as the ferry pulls away from
> the terminal, serving up a gorgeous view of the
> towers of Wall Street, silent and gleaming, a view
> that all but a few passengers ignore.

Not an awful description, but perfunctory, inert, and imprecise. What about that sunset? What sort of garbage? The above description makes the reader do all the heavy lifting.

We long for eye-candy; instead we get epithets ("gorgeous"). Furthermore, as written the scene unfolds, like the proverbial falling tree, in a vacuum, with no one there to experience or interact with it, a scene with no character(s)—which, if not altogether impossible, is a contradiction. That this is a first-person narrative only increases the author's obligation to evoke character with each line, to make this as much a description of the narrator as of the scenery.

Here, for better or worse, is what got published as part of the story "My Search for Red and Gray Wide-Striped Pajamas":

> I plan our dates for late in the afternoon, in time
> to watch the sun spatter downtown with gold dust.
> Smoke-colored gulls follow orange and black tugs.
> The towers of Wall Street pocked with twenty-four
> karat windows. It's strange seeing the city looming
> so giant and silent, the towers like stalagmites, the
> sky a Hollywood rear-screen projector fake. So
> much removed beauty, silent and majestic, while
> at our feet banana peels and bubbling scum float
> on brown, murky waves, and in the lounge behind
> us passengers swallow their daily dose of shouting
> headlines (I swear, some people live for news-
> print). Only the tourists pretend to see the skyline.

10. SYMBOLISM

Symbolism is using one image to represent another. Symbols help to focus the themes of our novels and stories. One of the most famous literary symbols is the green lantern that shines at the end of Daisy Buchanan's dock in F. Scott

Fitzgerald's *The Great Gatsby*:

> As I sat brooding on the old, unknown world, I
> thought of Gatsby's wonder when he first picked
> out the green light at the end of Daisy's dock. …
> Gatsby believed in the green light, the orgiastic
> future that year by year recedes before us.

Green for envy? For money? For greed? For starboard?
Green as in "the grass is always greener on the other side?"
Green for greener pastures, for the hope of a brighter future? Whatever its intended meaning, the image sticks to
our ribs. Fitzgerald knew this, and so he chose to end his
novel with this striking image.

Symbols should never be forced into our work. Write
skillfully, diligently, honestly and truthfully, and you'll produce symbols naturally, as if by accident—though Freud
would remind us that, when it comes to tapping the unconscious, there's no such thing as an accident.

11. SOMETIMES A TREE IS JUST A TREE

Then again, some things don't need describing. *Never state
what's implied.*

And don't imply what's stated, either.

For a last word on description I give you Robert Hogan,
late professor emeritus at the University of Delaware:

> Twenty inglorious Miltons looked at a tree and
> saw God,
> Noted its "clutching fingers groping in the sod,"

[149]

Heard "Zephyr's gentle breezes wafting through
    her hair"
Saw "a solemn statue," heard "a growing woody
    prayer,"
Saw "dancing skirts" and "the Lord's design,"
"Green arrows to God" instead of pine,
Saw symbols in squirrels, heard musings in bees;
None of the Miltons saw any trees.

CHAPTER VI:
Scene, Summary & Flashback

*"We are all like Scheherezade's husband in that
we all like to know what happens next."*
—E.M. Forster

VI. SCENE, SUMMARY & FLASHBACK

Drama, or dramatic writing, gives fiction its pulse. And the heart of dramatic writing is the scene. The word comes from the Latin *scena*, or stage, by way of the Greek word for a temporary shelter or tent that forms the background for a dramatic performance. Similarly, the scenes in our stories provide a kind of housing or shelter for the dramatic moments they embody. Without scenes, your stories will be at best synoptic, at worst bald abstractions. Either way they will be left out in the cold.

A scene is an occurrence or incident or event. Simply, it is what happens next, and what happens after that. What we remember most in great stories are the scenes. They are what Scheherezade spins under threat of death.

There are two ways of conveying scene, through narrative exposition or summary, or dramatically, with moments rendered vivid and immediate mainly through dialogue and action, but also through descriptions of gestures, atmosphere and setting. Summary is expedient, dramatic scene elaborate; summary *tells*, dramatization *shows*. While narrative summary gives us a report about characters and their actions and movements, dramatic scene *reproduces* those actions so we experience them for ourselves, as if we are there.

A reader's participation in a story is always greater during a dramatized scene. Gatsby flinging his collection of silk shirts "in many colored disarray" to impress Daisy—that's a dramatized scene. Zorba bursting into the *taverna*, strutting up to the narrator and saying, "Taking me with you?"—that's a scene. Rose of Sharon breastfeeding the dying old man at the close of *The Grapes of Wrath*—that's a scene.

Summary has its benefits, too. For one thing, it takes up less space. And it takes less time and effort to write.

1. FROM SUMMARY TO DRAMATIC SCENE

Narrative's flexible suitcases, scenes hold not just action and dialogue (their prime constituents), but summary, description, background, stream-of-consciousness—even other scenes, or flashbacks—in short, all the components of narrative writing. Assume in your writing that you are always either in the middle of writing a scene, or writing your way into one.

Let's revisit a novel with a traditional opening in which summary funnels us into the first dramatic scene. Hemingway's *The Sun Also Rises* begins:

> Robert Cohn was once middleweight boxing champion of Princeton. Do not think that I am very much impressed by that as a boxing title, but it meant a lot to Cohn. He cared nothing for boxing, in fact he disliked it, but he learned it painfully and thoroughly to counteract the feeling of inferiority and shyness he had felt on being

> treated as a Jew at Princeton. There was a certain
> inner comfort in knowing he could knock down
> anybody who was snooty to him.

From here we're given more of Cohn's background, his shyness and discomfort on being treated as a Jew in Princeton, how he was a member of wealthy New York family; prepped at military school; nice boy; married five years; three children; lost inheritance; unhappy with rich wife (who ran off with painter of miniatures); divorced: taken in hand by new woman, Frances; discovered writing; wrote novel; panned by critics; goes to Europe, meets narrator in Paris ... Three pages later:

> I first became aware of his lady's attitude toward
> him one night after the three of us had dined to-
> gether. We had dined at l'Avenue's and afterward
> went to the Cafe de Versailles for coffee. We had
> several fines after the coffee, and I said I must be
> going. Cohn had been talking about the two of
> us going off somewhere on a weekend trip. He
> wanted to get out of town and get in a good walk.
> I suggested we fly to Strausbourg and walk up to
> Saint Odile, or somewhere or other in Alsace. ...

From pure generalized background the opening has led us to the summary of a scene. With the very next line Hemingway shifts from summary to dramatization. We have set foot in the scene.

> "I know a girl in Strasbourg who can show us the
> town," I said.
> Somebody kicked me under the table. I thought
> it was accidental and went on: "She's been there

> two years and knows everything there is to know
> about the town. She's a swell girl."
>
> I was kicked again under the table and, look-
> ing, saw Frances, Robert's lady, her chin lifting and
> her face hardening.
>
> "Hell," I said, "why go to Strasbourg? We could
> go up to Bruges, or to the Ardennes."
>
> Cohn looked relieved. I was not kicked again.

Though it takes him a while, Hemingway finally plants us firmly in a dramatized moment. We are there, with the narrator, sitting in a Parisian cafe getting our chins kicked. I would argue that this scene was in the back of Hemingway's mind from page 1, that all of the summary leading to it is by way of setting us up properly to have the scene deliver the maximum emotional punch (or kick, as it were).

Though it took several pages to get to the dramatized event, to its dialogue and action, I will argue that the scene as a whole begins with the words, "Robert Cohn was once middleweight boxing champion of Princeton."

In your own writing be conscious of when and how you shift from summary to dramatic scene and vice versa. The transitions should be seamless, with summary preparing us for action and action illustrating or embodying what has been summarized.

2. Choosing and Shaping Scenes

> *"Having worked out the general approach to his
> story, the writer is then ready to start figuring out
> his scenes. By the rule of elegance and efficiency, he
> will choose the smallest number of scenes possible."*
> —John Gardner, *The Art of Fiction*

I love that "rule of elegance and efficiency." *The Great Gatsby* consists of only a dozen or so judiciously selected scenes, resulting in a lyrical work fleshed out with poetic prose to maximum lushness. By contrast, Dicken's *Great Expectations* whips us through fifty-nine chapters and hundreds of scenes, an epic approach that spares little, but is no less entertaining. You must choose between approaches: minimal or maximal; lyric or epic; lean or fat.

Or something in-between.

Like a story in miniature, a scene has its own miniplot, a build-up to some sort of climax or resolution. The climax needn't be earth-shattering. In a scene in which Jack asks Jill to marry him, her answer resolves the scene and serves as its climax. In one where Toby must get home in time to feed his stroke-victim father, once he gets home, for better or worse, the tension is resolved; the scene has fulfilled its purpose, and it's time to start building toward the next crisis. When Daisy reacts to Gatsby's silk shirt display with delight and reverence, that scene ends.

Another type of climax within scene: After a long separation, two characters are reunited for the first time. Let's say they have been lovers. The resolution or climax of this reunion scene (which, properly constructed, should include all necessary background information) could be a warm hug or handshake, an impassioned embrace, or a slap in the face—or both characters walking past each other without saying a word.

A story (and even in rare cases a novel) may consist of a single scene. Hemingway's "A Clean, Well-Lighted Place" takes place in a café at closing time, with everything conveyed through the dialogue of two waiters, without recourse to flashback or summary.

Alternatively, a story may consist of any number of causally related scenes. I emphasize *causally related,* because if the scenes don't really have anything to do with each other or don't contribute to the story's overall theme and outcome, they may not belong in the story at all. To be strict about it, nothing in a work of fiction should be arbitrary or incidental. A scene, for instance, in which a fight breaks out in a bar where a man and a woman have stopped for a drink and to discuss whether or not to continue their love affair, must be labeled gratuitous unless the bar fight somehow altars their destiny. It might make them decide, for instance, that the world is a cold, brutal place and that they had better go home to their spouses; or that it's a cold, brutal place and they should go back to their hotel room and make more love.

3. PACING

A skilled author layers dramatic scene with summary, weaving and blending the two, aware that the best narratives are like roller coaster rides, with slow climbs of exposition (summary) leading to swift-reading dramatic scenes. You have experienced, I'm sure, that heavy feeling in your gut when you flip through a novel and find that it consists entirely of industrial-strength paragraphs, each a half city block long, with no relief in the form of direct dialogue. Such books take a long time to read and demand far more effort from us. Novels packed with action and dialogue read quickly.

The paradox being this: that though long blocks of exposition make for a sluggish read, plot-wise exposition can also speed things up. *Ten years later, the war was over and Isabella found herself homeless again.* That's exposition hurling us forward through time, accomplishing in a sentence a novel's worth of dramatic scenes.

In *Sense and Sensibility*, Jane Austen moves nimbly from scene to summary:

> Edward had been staying several weeks in the house before he engaged much of Mrs. Dashwood's attention. … She was first called to observe and approve him further by a reflection which Elinor chanced one day to make on the difference between him and his sister. It was a contrast which recommended him most forcibly to her mother.
>
> "It is enough," said she, "to say that he is as unlike Fanny is enough. It implies everything amiable. I like him already."
>
> "I think you will like him," said Elinor, "when you know more of him."
>
> "Like him!" replied her mother with a smile. "I can feel no sentiment of approbation inferior to love."
>
> "You may esteem him."
>
> "I have never yet known what it was to separate esteem and love."
>
> Mrs. Dashwood now took pains to get acquainted with him. Her manners were attaching and soon banished his reserve.

In the block of text above—chosen at random from

the novel—we begin with summary and generalization—a sort of synopsis or brief on the situation the characters find themselves in at this point in the chronology of the story. This synopsis gives way to a sampling of a particular conversation relevant to the situation—a bit of aural evidence, if you like (it could have been visual as well). Following a brief exchange of dialogue (scene), Austen—wanting to fast-forward her plot—reverts to summary mode.

How we combine scene and summary determines the *pacing* and *rhythm* of our writing, as well as its ultimate style and what sort of readers will be drawn to it.

What mixture to use? You choose. There are many ways to build a rollercoaster. While one author (Elmore Leonard) favors dramatic scene over summary, another (Jens Christian Grondahl) eschews all direct dialogue and most action. When we call a work of fiction "fast paced," that's a quantitative—not a qualitative—judgment. Writing fiction isn't the Indy 500. Sometimes slow and steady wins the race.

Not enough of an answer? How about this: *Write the sort of book you want to read.*

4. DIGRESSIONS AND FLASHBACKS

The skillful writer who has a story to tell and aims his exposition toward a particular moment or moments can get away with a lot of exposition: description, flashback, memories, reveries—even long flights of pure stream of consciousness. Books like Malcolm Lowry's *Under the Volcano* and Joyce's *Ulysses* owe much of their originality and depth to this last technique, while owing their readability (such as it is) to the flexibility of scene, to its ability to absorb details and elaboration while maintaining some tension. Distilled to their plots, Joyce's and Lowry's novels would each shrink to a few dozen pages. But to a scanty armature of scenes each author has heaped on the clay of his characters' interior lives, and what might otherwise have been modest novellas or stories have burgeoned (or bloated, according to taste) into epic, universe-grappling novels.

> *"It is never possible for a novelist to deny time inside the fabric of a novel: he must cling* however er lightly *to the thread of his story, he must touch the interminable tapeworm, otherwise he becomes unintelligible."*
> —E. M. Forster

The emphasis on the words *however lightly* is mine, and applies well to books like Lowry's, which have little or no dramatic action. And though Forster uses the word *story,* he might have said scene, since a story is always either a single long scene or a chain of scenes.

But when the thread breaks, dislodging narrative from any kind of scene, even our most vivid descriptions go begging, while our characters wander the stage like actors in search of a play. Limbs cut off from their blood supply, our hardest-worked passages go cold, shrivel, and die. We call the gangrenous result a digression: a passage that snatches us so irrevocably out of a moment that, like lovers interrupted mid-coitus, we never return to it wholeheartedly.

A flashback is a digression that works. And most digressions don't; they break the backs of the scenes they're meant to ride on. If, after reading four paragraphs describing the gin roses on Uncle Ed's cheeks, the reader forgets the prior scene in which he bursts into the parlor with a meat cleaver intent on castrating his dissolute nephew, something has gone very wrong indeed. Like an errant caboose, the flashback has come uncoupled. It is no longer part of the scene, but a distraction from it.

Yet when handled expertly even long flashbacks holding not just one but multiple scenes can work, and not just well, but superbly. Why do they work? How do they work? What keeps them from being digressive?

To find out, let's take a tour through one elaborate and beautifully constructed flashback.

5. ANATOMY OF A FLASHBACK: A GUIDED TOUR

In his brilliant early novel, *The Centaur,* John Updike interrupts a tense, carefully built-up scene in which Peter, his adolescent narrator-protagonist, is being driven to school on a snowy winter morning by his self-deprecatory father who teaches history there. He does so to take readers on a sidetrip to New York, a detour that burns up seven-hundred and fifty words (roughly three pages), and bores through no fewer than six distinct layers or levels of time.

Such long, complicated flashbacks are sometimes called "portmanteau," after those Victorian suitcases of leather or cloth that carried so much. But before we get to the flashback, let's dip into the main scene itself, during which, despite their tardiness and its potentially grave consequences, Peter's father picks up a hitchhiker. Space prevents my quoting Updike entire. Here is my truncation:

> "I was living with a guy up in Albany," the
> hitchhiker said reluctantly. …
> … "A friend?" [my father asked.]
> "Yeah. Kinda."
> "What happened? He pull the old double-
> cross?"
> In his delight the hitchhiker lurched forward be-
> hind me. "That's right, buddy," he told my father.
> "That's just what the fucking sucker did. Sorry,
> boy."

On behalf of his son, dad accepts the apology, adding
that Peter "hears more horrible stuff in a day than I have
in a lifetime." We are still in the main or primary scene.
Updike has gone to great pains to construct a tense situation in which the consequences of his characters' tardiness
are well established (Peter risks suspension; his father risks
losing his job). With the reader's involvement thus secured,
Updike has not only bought himself some narrative slack,
he's obliged to milk things a bit. Hence the hitchhiker, a
benevolent digression—benevolent for the reader, but not
to poor Peter:

> … I vividly resented that [my father] should even
> speak of me to this man, that he should dip the
> shadow of my personality into this reservoir of
> slime. That my existence at one extremity should
> be tangent to Vermeer and at the other to the
> hitchhiker seemed an unendurable strain.

Will the hitchhiker turn out to be truly evil? Will Vermeer-smitten Peter and his father get to school on time? If not, will Peter be suspended? Will his father get fired? All this Updike gives us to chew on. As if our teeth aren't busy enough, he tosses us a flashback.

But unlike dogs, readers are fussy: They won't chase any bone. Our flashbacks should have some meat on them, and more: They should be motivated.

Since long before Proust bit into that tea-soaked cookie, authors have used mnemonics—sensory phenomena that assist or help to assist memory—to motivate flashbacks. Rather than write (in essence), "For no good reason at all, Jack remembered the time when..." they use material within the primary scene as kindling to fuel their flashbacks. Updike being Updike, he does so brilliantly:

> ... But relief was approaching. ... We passed a trailer truck laboring toward the crest so slowly its peeling paint seemed to have weathered in transit. Well back from the road, Rudy Essick's great brown mansion sluggishly climbed through the downslipping trees.

Here comes the flashback. Note how nimbly Updike slips into it by means of not one but two mnemonics, first a sign, then a smell. The best flashbacks are always motivated by sensory stimuli.

> Coughdrop Hill took its name from its owner, whose coughdrops ("SICK? Suck an ESSICK!") were congealed by the million in an Alton factory

> that flavored whole blocks of the city with the
> smell of menthol. They sold, in their little tan-
> gerine-colored boxes, throughout the East; the
> one time in my life I had been to Manhattan, I
> had been astonished to find, right in the throat of
> Paradise, on a counter in Grand Central Station, a
> homely ruddy row of them.

From a strip of wintry Pennsylvania road we're transported to a cough drop factory, and to what I'll call level
two of Updike's scene, level one being the primary ride-to-
school scene in which the flashback is embedded. Note the
sly insertion of that *had been*, the past perfect tense, which
tells us, lest there be any confusion, that we've dipped into
another layer of time.

When writing in the past tense, to obviate a flashback
dip into the past perfect. Once having established the tem-
poral shift, you can drop the perfect tense—as Updike does
promptly. From here the flashback descends, elevator-like,
through layers of scene. The same paragraph continues:

> In disbelief I bought a box. Sure enough, on the
> back, beneath an imposing miniature portrait
> of the factory, the fine print stated MADE IN
> ALTON, PA. And the box, opened, released the
> chill, ectoplasmic smell of Brubaker Street. The
> two cities of my life, the imaginary and the
> actual, were superimposed; I had never dreamed
> that Alton could touch New York. I put a cough-
> drop into my mouth to complete this delicious
> confusion and concentric penetration; my teeth
> sweetened and at the level of my eyes, a hollow
> mile beneath the ceiling that on an aqua sky

> displayed the constellations with sallow electric
> stars, my father's yellow-knuckled hands wrung
> together nervously through my delay. I ceased to
> be impatient with him and became as anxious as
> he to catch the train home.

The elevator has dropped to level three, to a scene in which father waits as son buys a box of cough drops in Grand Central Station. The difference between level two and level three is one of immersion. Level two is where we transition, abstractly, to New York in the line, "I had been astonished to find, right in the heart of Paradise ... a homely, ruddy row of them." This and the next several lines tell us about being in Grand Central, but then, seamlessly, we're *there*, in an actual, vivid scene: hence level three. A minor scene, true, but a scene, leading us deeper into the flashback.

Same paragraph:

> Up to this moment my father had failed me.
> Throughout our trip, an overnight visit to his
> sister, he had been frightened and frustrated. The
> city was bigger than the kind he understood. The
> money in his pocket dwindled without our buy-
> ing anything. Though we walked and walked, we
> never reached any of the museums I had read of.
> The one called the Frick contained the Vermeer of
> the man in the big hat. ...

The above passage has us in level four, wherein the New York trip is first broadly summarized. From there the focus tightens on Peter's devoutly wished-for encounter with his two favorite paintings by Vermeer.

> That these paintings, which I had worshipped in reproduction, had a simple physical existence seemed a profound mystery to me: to come within touching distance of their surfaces, to see with my eyes the truth of their color, the tracery of the cracks whereby time had inserted itself like a mystery within a mystery, would have been for me to enter a Real Presence so ultimate I would not have been surprised to die in the encounter.

Arguably we've descended to level five, Updike having sketched a conjectural scene in which boy confronts Dutch Master. On this illusion the following short, blunt sentence comes down like a sledgehammer:

> My father's blundering blocked it.

If the rules of Fiction 101 say, "never put a flashback in a flashback," Updike's hammer does a good job of smashing that, too. Having paid this hypothetical visit to Vermeer's masterpieces, we're now reeled back into the hotel room where Peter's been stuck the whole time.

> We never entered the museums; I never saw the paintings. Instead I saw the inside of my father's sister's hotel room [Level five]. Though suspended twenty stories above the street, it smelled strangely like the lining of my mother's fur-collared winter coat. Aunt Alma sipped a yellow drink and dribbled the smoke of Kools from her very thin red lips. She had white, white skin and her eyes were absolutely transparent with intelligence.

[166]

Though they belong to a flashback, the details here are as rich as can be; nothing is spared. Well, almost nothing.

> They talked all evening of pranks and crises in a vanished Passaic parsonage whose very mention made me sick and giddy, as if I were suspended over a canyon of time. Down on the street, twenty stories below, the taxi lights looped in and out.

Within a flashback it's best to avoid direct dialogue in favor of summarized or indirect dialogue. Dialogue broken into paragraphs undermines not only a flashback's integrity but its humility, suggesting that the flashback has staged a palace coup and usurped the primary scene.

> During the day, Aunt Alma, here as an out-of-town children's clothes buyer, left us to ourselves. The strangers my father stopped on the street resisted entanglement in his earnest, circular questioning.

Here (still in the same paragraph) Updike switches gears again, backtracking to the day that has led to this evening in the hotel, level four again. From there the elevator goes express, ascending up through generalities:

> Their rudeness and his ignorance humiliated me, and my irritation had been building toward a tantrum that the coughdrop dissolved.

Back to the scene in Grand Central Terminal. Did your ears pop? No wonder, since we're back on level two!

> I forgave him. In a temple of pale brown marble

Chapter VI

I forgave him and wanted to thank him for conceiving me to be born in a county that could insert its candy into the throat of Paradise. We took a subway to Pennsylvania Station and caught a train and sat side by side as easy as twins all the way home, and even now, two years later, whenever in our daily journey we went up or down Coughdrop Hill, there was for me an undercurrent of New York and the constellations that seemed to let us soar, free together of the local earth.

Note that all this time we've been in the same paragraph, one in which even Mr. Updike doesn't risk breaking into full-blooded, dramatized scene. Throughout the flashback we've been listeners, not spectators. Once transported via flashback into a new dramatic scene containing direct (as opposed to summarized) action and dialogue, the reader typically either forgets the primary scene or resents the bait and switch. When this happens it may indicate that our primary scene is in fact a *framing device*, a vessel into which we've poured the story we *really* wanted to tell. Such framing devices tend to be awkward and unnecessary, and suggest two remedies: (1) get rid of the frame; or (2) lose the painting and make the frame the subject.

Can flashbacks bloom successfully into full-flowered scenes without breaking the back of the present action? In highly skilled hands perhaps, sometimes. But even when handled as skillfully as possible some readers will find such flashbacks intrusive.

Back to Updike's flashback, which finally and literally, with a fresh paragraph of two sentences, screeches to a halt, landing us back on level one:

> Instead of braking, my father by some mistake
> plunged past the Olinger turnoff. I cried, "Hey!"

From here the primary scene takes over again and goes on for nine more pages to its resolution. By now Updike knows he has exhausted the good faith (read: tension) accrued within the primary scene; he has milked it to the limit, and possibly beyond.

Does he get away with it? I say yes, but then I've read the scene in its entirety and within its context; you haven't. That Updike writes some of the best prose in any language doesn't hurt, either.

If you don't write like Updike and want to avoid any risk of digression, the one sure way is to keep flashbacks short.

> Coughdrop Hill took its name from the factory
> that flavored whole blocks with its product. One
> time, in New York City, I was astonished to find a
> box of them for sale in Grand Central Station. The
> trip had been a disaster. Thanks to my father we
> never saw any of the museums I'd longed to see.
> We spent the whole time holed up in my aunt's
> stuffy hotel room where, while she and my father
> blabbed away, I watched the traffic through her
> twentieth floor window. I was so pissed I didn't
> speak to my father all the way home.

Beyond brevity my version has nothing over Updike's; in fact it's markedly inferior. Yet it carries the same basic information. My point being that you can say a lot in one short paragraph.

Another solution is to avoid flashbacks entirely. The

burden of our narratives—and on Sheherezade's head—is one of forward movement. By all means use flashbacks, but for good reason, not because you want to use them, but because your story *demands* them. Does the flashback deepen our understanding of a character or a relationship? Does it provide needed background?

In the end, it comes down to what a story needs.

And what will keep King Schariar's sword off our necks.

6. BENDING TIME, BREAKING THE RULES

Those of you wishing to subject yourselves to works that flout every single rule that I've set down here may wish to dip into Julio Cortázar's aforementioned *Hopscotch*, a novel consisting entirely of flashbacks—or flash-forwards, if you like, since the chapters may be read in any order.

Likewise in *Tristam Shandy* Lawrence Stern makes mincemeat of chronological time. At one point, having obtained our permission to digress for a half hour, he does so for five minutes longer, forcing him to accomplish "in five minutes less than no time at all" what his digression has left undone.

You may also want to pick up James Joyce's *Finnegan's Wake*, with this warning: since the novel has no beginning or ending—or rather, since the beginning *is* the ending and vice-versa—you may never put it down.

For the less intrepid, I recommend Michael Ondaatje's *The English Patient*, specifically the sections where the spy Caravaggio turns up (though the whole novel is infused with flashbacks).

Then there's that early flashback in *Lolita*, in which

Humbert's fixation with Annabel, the ur-Lolita, is recalled.

No survey of flashbacks is complete without *The Great Gatsby*, which holds at least two great ones, including the one where we learn how Daisy and Gatsby first met.

7. TO BE REMEMBERED—MAKE A SCENE

When I get feedback on my stories, I'm always delighted to hear that someone found a character likeable or interesting, or that a description has painted an indelible image in someone's mind, or that I've got a timely theme by the tail, or that my style fits perfectly into someone else's ears.

But what I'm really hoping to hear is: "That scene where so-and-so did such-and-such? *That was a really good scene!*"

CHAPTER VII:
VOICE & STYLE

*"Human speech is like a cracked kettle on which
we tap crude rhythms for bears to dance to, while
longing to make music to melt the stars."*
—Gustave Flaubert

VII. VOICE & STYLE

1. VOICE VS. STYLE: WHAT'S THE DIFFERENCE?

"Just as all great music at heart comes from dance, so the living sentence comes from breath." So writes Donald Newlove in *First Paragraphs*, the first of his three handbooks "for the soul":

> We write to a rhythm of breathing. A line must breathe. On bad days we choke our line with headstuff and try to slap life into stillborn wordage. On bad days we chop thoughts into lengths like so much hemp or clothesline. On good days these chords magically begin to breathe. Our lines slither and strike upward and infect. We are dangerous.

If style is a writer's personal aesthetic as reflected by her choice of themes and overall approach in presenting them, then voice is the particular tone adopted in telling a specific story. Carson McCullers has a distinct style that veers toward—and often plunges into—the macabre, and which embraces her entire oeuvre. Through it we recognize anything that she writes as distinctly hers. That said, each of McCullers' short stories, novels, and plays has its own unique voice, dictated by specific characters and situations.

As proof I offer the following excerpts from two of Mc-Culler's novels, the first from *The Heart is a Lonely Hunter*, the second from *Reflections in a Golden Eye:*

> In the town there were two mutes, and they were always together. Early every morning they would come out from the house where they lived and walk arm in arm down the street to work. The two friends were very different.

> The late autumn sun laid a radiant haze over the new sodded winter grass of the lawn, and even in the woods the sun shone through places where the leaves were not so dense, to make fiery golden patterns on the ground. Then suddenly the sun was gone. There was a chill in the air and a light, pure wind. It was time for retreat. From far away came the sound of the bugle, clarified by distance and echoing in the woods with a lost hollow tone. The night was near at hand.

What I call voice is sometimes also referred to as diction or tone. Essentially, they are one and the same. Stendhal famously wrote to Balzac that "While composing the *Chartreuse*, to acquire the [desired] tone, I used to read two or three pages of the *code civil* every morning." Similarly writers from Melville to Steinbeck and Morrison have scavenged the King James Bible in search of lofty rhythms for their prose.

The voice in Salinger's *A Catcher in the Rye* differs from that in *Seymour: An Introduction*. Still, we might guess that both works are by the same author, since they share the same style.

Saul Bellow's *Seize the Day* begins:

> When it came to concealing his troubles, Tommy Wilhelm was not less capable than the next fellow. So at least he thought, and there was a certain amount of evidence to back him up.

The voice here is calm, tinged with ironic understatement. We read that "not less capable" with a dubious raised eyebrow, and the "So at least he thought" seals our doubts. This is the story of a world-class loser told with wry, deadpan elegance in a voice that has little in common with that of the narrator of Bellow's most famous work, *The Adventures of Augie March:*

> I am an American, Chicago born—Chicago, that somber city —and go about things as I have taught myself, free-style, and will make the record in my own way: first to knock, first admitted; sometimes an innocent knock, sometimes a not so innocent. But a man's character is his fate, says Heraclitus, and in the end there isn't any way to disguise the nature of the knocks by acoustical work on the door or gloving the knuckles.

Like the city of Augie's birth, this voice is Big and Blustery, swaggering through its sentences with sleeves rolled up and necktie loose. But the *style* in both cases, with its loosened-tie informality, is unmistakably Bellow's.

[175]

CHAPTER VII

Or take these two openings:

> Gerard Maines lived across the hall from a
> woman named Benna, who four minutes into any
> conversation always managed to say the word
> penis. He was not a prude, but, nonetheless, it
> made him wince.

> Meet in expensive beige raincoats, on a pea-
> soupy night. Like a detective movie. First, stand
> in front of Florsheim's Fifty-seventh Street win-
> dow, press your face close to the glass, watch
> the fake velvet Hummels inside revolving around
> the wing tips; some white shoes, like your father
> wears, are propped up with garlands on a small
> mound of chemical snow.

Both openings were written by Lorrie Moore, the first
from her novel, *Anagrams,* the second from her short story, "How to be an Other Woman." The first voice is the
more objective. The second, with its wisecracks, is sardonic,
in your face. Bridging both voices is the author's cunning,
faintly sadistic, mildly perverse humor.

Though each voice is cut to suit its characters, situa-
tions and themes, close reading reveals common traits, like
Moore's razor-sharp eye for contemporary details, and her
Flaubertian passion for *le mot juste.*

Though like an impersonator's Moore's voice may vary
from work to work, her style remains fixed as a bright star in
the evening sky. It matures; it evolves. Yet it doesn't essentially change. Style is author; voice is character.

Here's Bridget Jones scribbling in her diary:

> Oh, why am I so unattractive? Why? Even a man
> who wears bumblebee socks thinks I am horrible.
> Hate the New Year. Hate everyone. Except Daniel
> Cleaver. Anyway, have got giant tray-sized bar of
> Cadbury's Dairy Milk left over from Christmas on
> dressing table, also amusing gin and tonic min-
> iature. And am going to consume them and have
> fag.
>   —Helen Fielding, *Bridget Jones's Diary*

Bridget's voice is sloppily urgent, skimping on articles and pronouns as befits a romantically obsessed young woman sprawled across her bedcovers in nightgown and fluffy slippers, jotting away.

Compare with:

> If you really want to hear about it, the first thing
> you'll probably want to know is where I was
> born, and what my lousy childhood was like, and
> how my parents were occupied and all before
> they had me, and all that David Copperfield kind
> of crap, but I don't feel like going into it, if you
> want to know the truth.
>   —J.D. Salinger, *The Catcher in the Rye*

Like many an adolescent before and since, Salinger's Holden Caufield is belligerent ("I don't feel like going into it"). The whole passage is written with the slump and smirk of a kid who's just been told to clean up his room. He'll do it when and if he feels like it. The same attitude that puts parents off pulls readers in. We're not used to being talked to quite like this, not on paper, anyway, and our attention is duly grabbed.

Nor are we apt to be spoken to this way daily:

> Call me Ishmael. Some years ago—never mind
> how long exactly—having little or no money in
> my purse, and nothing particular to interest me
> on shore, I thought I would sail about a little
> and see the watery part of the world. It is a way I
> have of driving off the spleen and regulating the
> circulation.
>
> —Herman Melville, *Moby-Dick* or *The Whale*

Ishmael isn't exactly belligerent, but he's sure got an attitude ("never mind how long exactly"). Like Bellow's Augie March, he's going to tell his story his own way, as he sees fit, deciding for himself what's none of your business and what is, not giving a damn whether or not you want to hear about his spleen.

Let's perform a ghoulish little experiment, shall we, and transplant the blood of Ishmael into Holden Caufield, and vice-versa. What would they sound like?

> Call me Holden. Around last Christmas—never
> mind when exactly—I decided to swim free of
> the brackish waters of the Pennsylvania prep
> school where I found myself slowly drowning.
> Wishing to see a more clamorous and glamorous
> part of the world, I paddled myself to Gotham,
> with its forests of concrete and steel. It's a way I
> have of shaking off depression, and escaping all
> those blazer-bedecked, prep-school phonies.

If you really want to hear about it, first thing you'll probably want to know all about my boring past, and how I decided to chuck it all and sail the seven seas, and how I got the job on the whaling ship and all that crap, but I really don't feel like going into it, if you really want to know the truth.

The experiment works, but then so did Dr. Frankenstein's, sort of. A Holden-style Ishmael would no sooner set off on a whaling ship than he'd fly to Pluto. And Ishmael-Holden, rather than mix with whores in hotels, would head for the nearest wharf and book passage on a slow boat to China. Style and subject can neither be artificially separated nor conjoined against their will.

Or they can, but with ghoulish results.

2. How Not to Have a Style

"All the fun is in how you say a thing."
—Robert Frost

Think of the way you walk, or talk. Do you think of them? As you're walking down the street, are you aware of your posture, the way your toes point, how far you swing your arms and hips? Do you cut your walk to fit the latest trends in locomotion? Do you walk like Marilyn Monroe, or talk like Brad Pitt? Hopefully you walk like no one but yourself, and you speak the same way, because—well, because that's who you are. So it is with style.

But why take my word for it when you can take Aristotle's: "Style is the man." Or Katherine Anne Porter's: "The style is you." Or E.B. White's: "Style results more from what a person is than from what he knows." Or Susan Sontag's: "Style is the principle of decision in a work of art, the signature of the artist's will."

One sure way to avoid having a style is to try too hard to have one. When we try to be anyone but ourselves, we fail. "You can cultivate a style, I suppose," said Katherine Porter. "But I should say it remains a cultivated style."

We fail, too, when we try to be all things to all people: to be both lush and lean; to write formally *and* casually (though somehow Bellow gets away with this); to be true to our characters' unsophisticated natures while parading our vast and arcane vocabularies. Try having it all, and you end up having nothing.

Style should be a result, not a means. It is hard-won personality, not a desperate last-minute *grab* at a persona, a stuck-on mask to show the world. A meek, tentative man isn't likely to write muscular prose. Nor is a stevedore apt to compose in baroque sentences any more than an effete Victorian will write like a stevedore.

Any earnest attempt to express oneself clearly, with no motive superceding that of communication, will likely result in a good style, one that's transparent and honest, that doesn't irritate or obfuscate. Often beginning writers put the style cart ahead of the story horse: in their eagerness to *have* a style they forget that true style emerges from character, and can't be forced, faked, or foisted upon us.

> My father is going to die today. I'm sitting on the
> bed next to him, leaning down, my forearm

propped against his. Our palms are pressed
together in a formal dance position. We stay that
way for a weird eternity. If he weren't in a coma,
I'd never dare do this. My father refused to dance
at his own wedding. And all the years after that.
My mother has never forgiven him.

The voice and style that reaches us in this opening paragraph of Joanna Torrey's novel *He Goes, She Goes* is at once
warm and cold, bitter and sweet, formed of simple, declarative sentences that nevertheless convey complex emotions
("If he weren't in a coma, I'd never dare do this."). Complexity of character and emotion needn't be mirrored by language. Sometimes, like still waters, simple and quiet words
runs deep.

Compare:

Landscape-tones: brown to bronze, steep skyline,
low cloud, pearl ground with shadowed oyster
and violet reflections. The lion-dust of desert:
prophet's tombs turned to zinc and copper at
sunset on the ancient lake. It's huge sand-faults
like watermarks from the air; green and citron
giving to gunmetal, to a single plum-dark sail,
moist, palpitant; sticky-winged nymph. Taposiris is
dead among its tumbling columns and seamarks,
vanished the Harpoon Men. … Mareotis under a
sky of hot lilac.
   —Lawrence Durrell, *Balthazar*

Gracious, what are we to make of this? In a single paragraph Lawrence Durrell has challenged my spell-checker
a half-dozen times. To what end all these hues splattered

across the page? Wherefore all this fancy footwork and filigree? Like a tot with his jumbo box of Crayola crayons, Durrell can't resist using every one of his forty-eight colors. Is he just showing off, throwing "headstuff" in our faces? Or does all this landscape painting serve a deeper purpose in the story he's telling?

Yes, and no. Durrell sets out intentionally to weave a Persian carpet of words—and succeeds through not just one novel, but a boxed set of four, comprising the famous (and now rarely read) *Alexandria Quartet*, wherein he snares not only ancient and modern Alexandria, but romantic love in all four dimensions—three of space and one of time. Sounds ambitious? I wouldn't try it. Does it work? Well, the result is certainly Byzantine in its complexity, and guaranteed to get you drunk on words—though you may need to *be* drunk to read it.

Now for a more contemporary, less exotic, voice:

> So let me dish you this comedy about a family I knew when I was growing up. There's a part for me in this story, like there always is for a gossip, but more on that later. …

Slangy, hip, familiar—Holden Caufield, but grown-up. I've chosen that word *hip* carefully, since the novel this comes from, Rick Moody's *The Ice Storm,* is set in the early seventies, when Richard Nixon was president, and string-bean casseroles, leisure suits, and key parties (parties where guests dropped their keys into a bowl, then left with each other's spouses) were the rage. Throughout Moody's guided tour through postrevolutionary suburban dysfunction, the narrator's voice remains staccato, cool, filled with sly sentence fragments and smarmy wordplay ("Fucking family. Feeble and forlorn and floundering and foolish and frustrating and functional and sad, sad."), while the book itself holds enough '70's lore to stuff a deluxe edition of Trivial Pursuit. As voices go, you may like or hate Moody's. But odds are you won't feel indifferent.

3. THE GOOD, THE BAD, THE BEAUTIFUL—AND THE OUTRAGEOUS

A mannered style is a bad style because it's faked or forced. Some would argue that Moody's style is mannered, that it's blowing "headstuff" at us. When the smoke clears we'll see what, if anything, Moody really has to say.

A mannered sentence:

> The burger delivery came in the form of a drop, with the bounce of the Styrofoam plate dislodging the top bun from its mark as a result.

What is this author saying, or trying to say? That the burger was dropped? That it bounced off a Styrofoam plate? That in falling its bun was dislodged? Here, the author has taken a relatively simple series of actions and, through convoluted wording, made it less than clear. Unless from a restaurant to a home no one thinks of a burger as something delivered, let alone delivered "in the form of a drop." What's more, thanks to the sentence's aggressively passive construction, it's hard to be sure who has delivered the burger to whom, or whether the deliverer has dropped the burger on purpose or it has fallen by accident. "Men," wrote Schopenhauer, "should use common words to say uncommon things, but they do the opposite." The attempt at linguistic novelty here is misguided.

Or is it? When it comes to rendering judgments on literary works, no area is more subjective than style. Faced with this sentence:

> There is a moonshaped rictus in the streetlamp's globe where a stone has gone and from this aperture there drifts down through the constant helix of aspiring insects a faint and steady rain of the same forms burnt and lifeless.

some readers will cheer while others will go ugh and throw Cormac McCarthy's *Suttree* into the nearest garbage receptacle. Me, I enjoy McCarthy's Thesaurus-raiding indulgences even as I am appalled by them.

There are those who think Shakespeare shoddy, Bernard Shaw and Samuel Johnson among them. On hearing that Shakespeare never once blotted a word, Johnson quipped, "Would that he had blotted a thousand!"

Can you read the later Henry James? I can't. Nor can I read much Faulkner without my guts getting as tangled up as his prose. And each time I try (again) to read Proust, I fall asleep reading about how he fell asleep—though it takes him many more pages. That doesn't make Proust a poor writer or me a poor reader. We simply have yet to find ourselves on the same page, so to speak.

When it comes to style, there's always room for argument. I happen to like *Under the Volcano;* many find it unreadable or a bore, a thin story padded with stream-of-consciousness navel-lint picking, which, to boot, succumbs to the sympathetic fallacy or the fallacy of imitative form (drunk writer writing about a drunken consul in drunken prose).

Something similar might be said of *Ulysses, Moby-Dick,* and almost any milestone classic of literature.

Ever read Gertrude Stein, or try to?

> As I was saying loving repeating being is in a way earthly being. In some it is repeating that gives to them always a solid feeling of being. In some children there is more feeling and in repeating eating and playing, in some in story-telling and their feeling. More and more in living as growing young men and women and grown men and women and men and women in their middle living, more and more there comes to be in them differences in loving repeating in different kinds of men and women, there comes to be in some more and in some less loving repeating.
>
> —Gertrude Stein, *The Making of Americans*

The best approach to such work is to imagine yourself living in 1908, and seeing Picasso's *Les Demoiselles d'Avignon* for the first time. Unlike most people of that era, you, being far more sophisticated, would naturally appreciate that work's revolutionary innovations and call it a masterpiece. The difference between Picasso's painting and Stein's *The Making of Americans* is that a painting takes a moment to look at, whereas, at a thousand pages, to admire Stein's novel takes considerably more endurance.

Unless you're content to write unpublishable works, when evolving a style you need to balance your own needs and aesthetics with those of your readers, keeping in mind that readers can be rude. Unless it's been assigned to them in a graduate course, nothing compels them to read your work. They hold all the cards. Somehow you have to appeal to them.

Here's a voice that, after 165 years, still appeals:

> There was no possibility of taking a walk that day.
> We had been wandering, indeed, in the leafless
> shrubbery an hour in the morning; but since
> dinner (Mrs Reed, when there was no company,
> dined early) the cold winter wind had brought
> with it clouds so sombre, and rain so penetrating,
> that further outdoor exercise was now out of the
> question.

Prim, proper, tightly-corseted, clearly of the Victorian age, an age when people "dined" and things were "out of the question." This is Charlotte Brontë speaking to us through her heroine, Jane Eyre, who is rescued—temporarily—from the fate of a governess by the dark, mysterious and faintly bestial Mr. Rochester.

A very different voice:

> Summer days began without a plan. You got up.
> You had a bowl of cereal. You went outside.
> A lawn mower hummed. Ducks passed over-
> head in perfect V formation like World War Two
> bombers. A dog barked, and another dog barked

back. Somebody was hammering nails into a
roof. Somebody was bounding a basketball three
streets away. You heard the sound, then the echo.
A cat crept across the grass and disappeared beneath a hedge. It was hot. The sun was strong.
　　—Dan Pope, *In the Cherry Tree*

In this passage and in his novel as a whole, Mr. Pope
captures almost perfectly the sunstruck world of suburban
adolescence. I say *almost* because that "beneath" bothers me,
when a kid would think "under." But that's a nitpick. Who
but an adolescent kid compares ducks in flight to World
War II bombers? The pubescent male tendency to leave no
disgusting stone unturned is evoked even more perfectly in
Pope's dialogue, as in this typical exchange:

"Do you know what this is?"
Tiger said, "Bicycle pump."
Stev said, "Wrong. This is the most unbeliev-
able farting machine ever created."
I said, "You won't believe it."
Stev said, "This is the best."
I said, "It's unbelievable."
Stev said, "Bend over."

I leave you to imagine the rest of this charming scenario. In Pope's writing, his style (clipped sentences, a high
percentage of monosyllabic words) serves the novel's voice,
which serves its theme.

Here's Kurt Vonnegut serving up tragedy on a global
scale with a weary sigh:

Chapter VII

> All this happened, more or less. The war parts,
> anyway, are pretty much true. One guy I knew
> really was shot in Dresden for taking a teapot that
> wasn't his. Another guy I knew really did threaten
> to have his personal enemies killed
> by hired gunmen after the war. And so on. I've
> changed all the names.

In this opening to Vonnegut's *Slaughterhouse-Five* or *The Children's Crusade*, humility and straightforwardness win us over. The author has no personal axe to grind, no need to embellish, wax poetic, or otherwise juice-up his tale, which is juicy enough. We can almost see Uncle Kurt sitting there, at his kitchen table with his pack of Pall Malls and a cup of coffee (laced with a little something, perhaps?), ready to tell his war story in a series of self-effacing shrugs and sighs. So it goes.

Here's Martin Amis who is anything but self-effacing:

> This is the story of a murder. It hasn't happened
> yet. But it will. (It had better.) I know the murder-
> er, I know the murderee. I know the time, I know
> the place. I know the motive *(her* motive), and I
> know the means. I know who will be the foil, the
> fool, the poor foal, also utterly destroyed. And I
> couldn't stop them, I don't think, even if I wanted
> to. The girl will die. It's what she always wanted.
> You can't stop people, once they *start*. You can't
> stop people, once they start creating.

If the narrator of Amis' *London Fields* is hand-wringingly giddy with the discovery of his plot and characters, we can't blame ourselves for suspecting that Amis himself may be under a similar giddy spell—giddy with his own talent. From every paragraph of *London Fields* that talent leaps out to lick our faces like an overzealous golden retriever. And like a golden retriever, Amis can't quite seem to help himself as he pants away, slapping his thick yellow tail against walls and furniture. Note how, through careful punctuation and italics, Amis directs our reading like a conductor conducting a symphony:

> I wish to Christ I could do Keith's voice. The *t's* are viciously stressed. A brief gutteral pop, like the first nanosecond of a cough or a hawk, accompanies the hard *k*. When he says *chaotic,* and he says it frequently, it sounds like a death rattle. 'Month' comes out as *mumf.* He sometimes says, "Im feory …" when he speaks theoretically, "There" sounds like *dare* or *lair.* You could often run away with the impression that Keith Talent is eighteen years old.

This is writing on steroids, writing that never lets you forget the author and how talented he is (is it merely—can it possibly be—coincidental that he names his protagonist/murderer "Talent"?). It's also extremely funny and imaginative and engaging if you can stand all that fur and saliva.

Rather than leap out and bite us with verbal pyrotechnics, Harper Lee gives the spotlight to Scout Finch, the eight-year-old narrator of her only novel, *To Kill a Mockingbird,* while Scout, in turn, lets her town, its weather and its people, take center stage:

> Maycomb was an old town, but it was a tired
> old town when I first knew it. In rainy weather
> the streets turned to red slop; grass grew on the
> sidewalks, the courthouse sagged in the square.
> Somehow, it was hotter then; a black dog suf-
> fered on a summer's day; bony mules hitched to
> Hoover carts flicked flies in the sweltering shade
> of the live oaks on the square. Men's stiff collars
> wilted by nine in the morning.

No face-licking, chest-thumping, button-holing or showing-off here. This is writing devoid of attitude and aggression, limpid as a meadow brook, quiet, clear, subservient to its subject. Is Lee a better writer than Amis? Most readers would probably say yes; most writers would probably say no. Still, it's for you to decide.

Some people like a stiff poke in the chest, and Amis' book is a supercharged masterpiece. Yet it's unlikely that sales of *London Fields* will reach, let alone exceed, *Mockingbird's* thirty-million-plus copies. A little humility goes a long way.

4. DON'T FORCE IT

I don't know what else to tell you about style other than to forget about it, to let it create itself. The more you think about it, the more likely you are to trip over your own dancing feet. Think instead of the story you want to tell. Focus on getting at the truth of your characters in their situations, and on putting us, your readers, in their shoes. Be as honest, fair, concrete and specific as possible, and you'll have a good style.

You'll decide, for instance (because your story is cinematic and driven by action and dialogue) to write a third-person limited narrative in present tense, using short, declarative sentences studded with active verbs, and hardly any adjectives, with descriptions pared to a bare minimum (Hemingway, "The Killers;" Dan Pope, *In the Cherry Tree)*. Or you'll write long, complex sentences, with lush, show-stopping descriptions, portmanteau flashbacks, torrid streams-of-conscience, and only a whisper of action here and there (Lowry, *Under the Volcano;* Woolf, *To the Lighthouse)*.

The choice isn't yours, but the story's.

One final caution regarding style. It can't be added after the fact like ketchup to an omelet. You can sharpen a slack or bloated style through editing. You can spruce up tired similes and spice up dull descriptions. You can improve what's already good. But if the overall style is mannered or forced, the best you can hope for is to cut your losses, and opt for an end result less obnoxious if more innocuous.

On the other hand, if you've written journalese, you can always try to pump some poetry into it, but your efforts may be too little, too late, and forced.

The best styles spring from character—our own characters, and from the characters we create. They not only tell readers how we write, they tell them who we are.

5. Genres and Literary Fiction

Science-fiction, romance, gothic, detective (or mystery), thrillers: each of these genres comes with its own particular set of rules and principles, some in opposition to the rules of "fine" or "literary" writing, not only allowing for but insisting upon a hefty dose of formula and cliché. In writing a romance novel, for instance, one is not only permitted to describe the heroine's eyes as emerald green, it's *de rigeur*.

Readers of most genre fiction aren't looking for fresh language or anything terribly innovating, surprising, or original, but for consistency. They aren't interested in provocative or challenging structures and styles, but in stories that fulfill a standardized list of expectations, that surprise us within their traditions and formulas, not by subverting or otherwise modifying them.

When writing in a genre, it's best to observe the conventions of that genre. Why give readers caviar when they want Cheez Whiz, or chopped liver? On the other hand, great works have resulted from writers coopting genres, as Paul Auster did in *City of Glass*, a detective novel dipped in surrealism, served with a side dish of absurdity. *A Clockwork Orange* is literary sci-fi with a dystopian twist. Hannah Tinti's short story "Home Sweet Home" is a literary whodunit that carves time into a jigsaw puzzle.

The best so-called literary fiction conflates or defies categorization. Joyce's *A Portrait of the Artist as a Young Man* is part memoir, part *bildungsroman*—a novel of education. It's also a treatise on Catholicism and art. Henry Miller's *Tropic of Cancer* is part cosmological rant, part portrait of the expatriate as a growling digestive system (with a few other organs tossed in). "A gob of spit in the face of God, man, destiny—what you will"—so Miller himself describes it.

The beauty of literary fiction is that, like all great art, it defies easy labels. For truly innovative contemporary works look to writers like Gilbert Sorrentino or David Markson. Markson's novels *(Readers Block, This Is Not a Novel)* document literary detritus and loss in epigrammatic sentences that somehow, through their cumulative effect, get to us deep under our skin—this despite that his novels, as such, have no stories, settings, characters, or dialogue.

> When I was their age I could draw like Raphael. But it took me a lifetime to learn to draw like they do.
> Said Picasso at an exhibition of children's art.

> A novel with no intimation of story whatsoever, Writer would like to contrive.

> And with no characters. None.

> The Globe Theater burned to the ground on June 29, 1613. Did any new play of Shakespeare's, not yet in quarto publication, perhaps burn with it?

From this short excerpt alone one might conclude than Markson's title for his work, *This is Not a Novel,* is apt. How dare he *not* offer this disclaimer! But don't forget that the word *novel* comes from the old French *nouvel,* or "modern," by way of the Latin word *novus,* meaning "new." Once upon a time a novel really was something new, a literary form that challenged existing, fusty forms, that flaunted the latest experiments and innovations: that dared to be different. Perhaps, then, Markson's title isn't so appropriate after all.

Perhaps he should have titled his book, *This Really is a Novel; the Rest are Frauds.*

6. STRANGE COMFORT AFFORDED BY THE PROFESSION: ON THE ECONOMICS OF STYLE

Among commercial publishers, however, books like *Reader's Block* grow increasingly rare. Writers with an avant garde bent should stand warned: Despite the noble (if often annoying) efforts of innovators like Fielding, Sterne, Woolf, Joyce, Proust, Stein, Beckett, these days the novel is hardly *new*. Face it, most novels published by commercial houses today all breathe the same stale, tried-and-true air.

That may be a factor of rude economics, with publishing houses run not as they once were, by gentle lovers of literature, but by corporate conglomerates who see no reason why books shouldn't be marketed like cars and deodorant. So they stick to tried-and-true formulas, recycling last years' hits, slapping new chrome on old models, betting everything on bestsellers, while forsaking everything in the middle or at the bottom of the list. Winner take all.

Unfortunately with this sort of thinking sooner or later everyone loses, starting with writers themselves and ending with the reading public—who, though the shelves at Barnes & Noble groan deceptively under the weight of millions of books, have fewer real choices in terms of the *kinds* of work reaching them. Ultimately, with marketing experts and corporate bean-counters serving as editors by proxy, all books start to sound like, well, books chosen by marketing experts and corporate bean-counters.

Then again, the writing "profession" may have to take some of the blame. With the flurry of graduate programs popping up like toadstools after a spring rain, each dedicated to conferring upon its graduates the equivalent of a literary driver's license, what was once an art has gone the way of law, medicine, and plumbing—has been professionalized. Which in no way serves literature, let alone art. That editors take such degrees seriously shows how quickly the disease has spread.

It also means that today's writers—rather than wrestle alone in their rooms with their demons—work by committee, in workshops among ten or fifteen of their fellows, gathering advice and opinions. All of which is good for one's social life, maybe, but not necessarily for one's craft or sullen art. The trouble with writing workshops (and I should know; I teach them) is that while at best they can instill raw talents with formal competence and prepare them for publication, at worst they can be great levelers, churning out dozens of competent, bland writers, writers whose voices are clever, clear, sharp, smooth—but who have little to say, nor any fresh way of saying it. Meanwhile the more daring students find themselves ostracized; or (and I've seen this more times than I can tell) they never get invited to the party: No MFA program will have them.

I don't want to denounce all graduate or other writing programs: Some of them are quite good. And as I said, at best they prepare writers for the rigors and challenges of publishing and for the writing life in general. In my years of teaching, I've watched many students evolve from amateurs to artists, and hope that I've contributed to that evolution.

CHAPTER VII

The danger is that instead of becoming artists students become professionals: regimentally indoctrinated careerists jumping through all the right hoops to land that first book deal (attend high-profile MFA program, write first novel on trendy subject in trendy prose, meet your agent waiting tables at Breadloaf, sign two-book deal, move "the Slope," be photographed by Sigrid Estrada sipping a cappuccino and chain-smoking Gauloises at Balthazar). The trouble with this program is that for each circus seal who makes it through all those hoops, a hundred others fail and lose their integrity—all an artist really has—in the process.

However you achieve it—alone in your garret or in a classroom—you're style should be you, nothing more or less, turned into words on paper: you're way of thinking, of feeling, of looking at the world. When you write it's you and no one else taking the plunge, swimming underwater and holding your breath.

With time, effort and luck, you'll cultivate strong muscles, capacious lungs, and a graceful, efficient stroke that lets you swim far and deep.

CHAPTER VIII:
THEME

*"I write because I don't know what I think
until I read what I say."*
—Flannery O'Connor

VIII. THEME

1. NEED TO KNOW

By seventh grade to our dismay most of us knew the word. We knew, too, that every book or story had one, buried like a pirate's treasure or a plum in a pie. Unless we dug it out, Mrs. Schnabel would get her paddle and beat us to within an inch of our lives. And so we grew to hate "theme" and everything it stood for.

We were taught to think of theme as synonymous with *message*: What is the author *trying* to say?—the implication being that the author had failed to get his message across, and it was up to Mrs. Schnabel and her motley crowd of seventh graders to come to his rescue. Like a little army of truffle-hunting boars we went to work, snouts buried in *Ethan Frome* and *The Scarlet Letter,* rutting out themes.

Grown writers, we need no longer fear Mrs. Schnabel's paddle. Nor is it our job to hide or seek messages in our work. That said, sooner or later, we must confront theme in its broadest sense and face the question *What are we writing about?*

Depending on how many words we've already committed to paper, the question may seem more or less impudent. However far along we are in the process, assuming that we've been following our artistic urges and instincts (as well we should), the question is bound to raise a few hackles, and may even in isolated cases provoke a nervous breakdown.

The reason is simple: We fiction writers don't always know what we're doing. Until we're done we never have the *whole* picture, only parts of it. This is especially true of novelists who can't reasonably be expected to hold the world of a novel, in all its richness and complexity, in their heads while writing it.

Like good lawyers, writers tend to learn what they must about their works-in-progress on a need-to-know basis, and to provide their readers with approximately the same level of awareness and information. Think of a novel as a mountain that author, readers and characters alike must climb, an Everest or Annapurna that promises a tantalizing and transcendent view of life and possibly even of the universe—a view that requires effort and struggle to reach. For the characters the struggle consists of conflict; for the reader it consists of having to carry, in the form of information, those supplies necessary to complete the journey; for the writer the struggle consists of knowing exactly what and how much information to dole out to the reader, and when. Give the reader too much to carry, and he won't complete the journey; give him too little, and he won't be able to appreciate the view from the top when he gets there.

But how much information must we writers have to make the journey? And when should we have it? In what form?

2. A GRAIN OF SAND

The moment we start writing, and even before we sit down to write, we have to know certain things. A pearl doesn't form inside an oyster without a grain of sand. And what we know varies from project to project.

Sometimes a sentence is enough to get started. A recent story of mine began with these words that came to me as I lay in bed, dazed from a dream: "Picasso cannot drive: he finds cars too amusing." That was all I needed to get started.

And though it was a strong enough start to propel me through an entire draft, I no sooner got to the end than I realized that what I'd written was not so much a story as a situation—a series of amusing moments built around and about the supposition that the artist Picasso, at the height of his fame, comes to California and engages a failed shoe salesman to chauffeur him on a pointless journey to Peru.

All of this, mind you, was arrived at pretty much by gut instinct. But gut instinct will only get you so far. A situation, even one elaborated into a series of lively but only tenuously related scenes, still lacks something essential to make it a strong story. It needs an organizing principle, something to bind its disparate parts together, a central notion or idea. A theme.

So, having written this "amusing" first draft, with its charismatic (thanks to Picasso, not me) main character and panoramic scenery, it was up to me, now, to figure out what that central idea was. What was my story about? What was my theme?

The answer lay nowhere else but in the story itself, in what I had written so far. All the clues I needed were there, presumably. So I put on my Sherlock Holmes hat, picked up the draft, and began my search with this in mind: The answer should come in the form of a short phrase or, better yet, a single word.

Why one word? Because it simplifies things. And the process of uncovering our themes is, at least in part, a process of simplification. Think of it as a mathematical problem. Presented with a number of fractions, you are asked to find their lowest common denominator, the smallest, non-zero number that can be shared by them all. With a story or a novel something of the like is at hand. Although your early drafts may present you with any number of disparate subjects and themes, dispersed through any number of episodes or scenes, like the proverbial umbrella, one theme must unify them all.

Your own methods of theme-stalking may vary, and may include going for long drives or walks, swimming, meditation, brooding, eating peanut butter standing up, straight from the jar with a knife. See yourself as a Jungian analyst, and your stories as dreams wanting interpretation. And know that the themes are already there—in our work as well as in our lives. We just have to seek and sort them out.

3. ORGANIC UNITY

In "The Importance of the Single Effect in a Prose Tale," an 1842 essay Edgar Allen Poe wrote in review of Nathaniel Hawthorn's *Twice-Told Tales,* Poe insists, "Without a certain continuity of effort—without a certain duration or repetition of purpose—the soul is never deeply moved."

Poe's essay may be read as a defense of the short story form as superior to poetry and the novel, and as such seems a bit self-serving, since Poe was primarily a short story writer. Still, it makes an important point: that in a successful work of prose narrative, plot, characters, atmosphere, tone, even individual word choices, all contribute to a singular effect.

The fancy term for this is *organic unity:* the organization of a story's elements—plot, characters, setting, conflict—around a single theme, such that they enhance, interact with, and inform that theme. With any well-designed machine, nothing is extraneous; all of the parts contribute to the whole. Motifs, leitmotifs, patterns and repetitions—these and other devices all add to this sense of unity.

Without a unifying theme or idea, it's almost impossible for a novel or story to have a form—almost impossible, I say, excepting that on rare occasions stories cohere by accident, or, if you prefer, by enchantment. This is rare, and rarer still when writers expect it. As for the novelist who presumes to be so blessed, she is likely not only to be disappointed, but to face the onerous if not hopeless task of whipping a mishmash of lovingly rendered scenes into a focused and meaningful narrative.

Examine any great or even good work of fiction and you'll see that all of its parts contribute in some way to an overall effect. The whole of Flaubert's *Madame Bovary* is constructed (like the aforementioned pearl) around the title character's romantic delusions born of her stultifying middle-class existence. Characters, setting, plot, point of view: All arise from or are chosen to illustrate this theme. Flaubert buries Emma Bovary alive in the dullest of provincial villages and saddles her with an equally dull marriage. Through the agency of a wealthy Lothario living next door, Flaubert awakens and galvanizes her romantic yearnings. To this volatile mixture he adds Emma's insolvency, her love of finery, a man who shares her romantic yearnings, and a cunning merchant who draws her deep into debt. Result: a tragedy constructed around a single theme, the futility and vulgarity of provincial life.

When did Flaubert arrive at his theme? If we believe his friend Maxime Du Camp, the gestation took place in a flash on an Algerian mountaintop, in a burst of inspiration so bright it made Flaubert cry out, "I've found it! Eureka! Eureka! I'll call it *Emma Bovary!*" The truth is probably more sober. However he arrived at it, Flaubert was crafty enough to make sure that his theme arose, or seemed to arise, organically out of his raw materials.

The idea is not to make your themes explicit, but to use them as an organizing principle for selecting and orchestrating, either in the editing stage or earlier, the materials of your story. "Life being all inclusion and confusion, and art being all discrimination and selection," as Henry James reminds us. We must select and discriminate, and theme gives us the basis for doing so.

4. FINDING THE CENTER

So, in my story about a failed shoe salesman driving Picasso from California to the snowy peaks of Peru, what might possibly be the unifying theme? Well, I've said already that

Picasso was at the height of his fame, and that the shoe salesman was a failure. So, might the theme have to do with success and/or failure?

Indeed, this *was* the theme, or so I concluded, and went to work making sure that every moment in the story in some way illuminated it. If not, the moment had to be jettisoned, or rewritten. Its theme thus shored up, the finished product evolved from a series of colorful anecdotes to a real, solid story *about* something.

Not long ago a student of mine wrote the first lovely pages of a story, but didn't know where to go from there. She didn't know where to go because, though it stared her in the face, she didn't recognize her theme. The narrator, sixteen-year-old Becky, lives with her widower father, a collector of clocks, who has invited a younger friend of his college days for a weekend visit. The father—as indicated by all those clocks—is "a man of precision and preparation" who feels in control of his world. The friend, Rick, on the other hand, rides a motorcycle and "smells of anise" and is a sweaty slob. From Becky's descriptions of him she clearly finds him gross and grotesque, but just as clearly she is intrigued. As drafted the story stopped, as opposed to ending, with Becky going to sleep.

How to arrive at the story's real ending? Through its theme, which was obvious enough at least to this back seat driver. Though it may be about other things too, a story loaded with clocks had to be about time: that's the one word.

Having reached this conclusion, I looked back at the author's title page and saw the root of the problem. The story's working title? "Sweet Onion"—a title that in no way related to the strongly suggested theme (unless meant to connote the onion-like layering of time—a stretch). Perhaps the author knew something I didn't know, but her inability to finish her story told me otherwise. In fact the title revealed—as titles often do—that the author hadn't found the story's true center. Often our working titles supply us with our stories' themes, or make it clear that we don't yet know what they are. (Which is why you should title your stories provisionally, even in the earliest stages of writing, since the effort will help you locate the story's center.)

Specifically, the story was about a father losing his grip on time as implied by his daughter's sexual awakening. As we discussed the story it seemed clear to both my student and I that something more than sleep had to occur in this house full of clocks. Perhaps the narrator slips into Rick's room (her mother's former bedroom, maybe, since her parents hadn't slept together in years); or maybe sweaty Rick slips into *her* bedroom. Or she's caught by her father touching herself as she watches Rick sleep. But something must happen to fulfill the story's theme and demonstrate how all of dad's tightly wound clocks can't stop or even slow the advance of his daughter's sexuality: He must lose her soon, and she in turn will escape his ticking fortress.

When we write honestly about the things that obsess us, we can't help producing works that are thematically rich and even loaded. The trick is being able to recognize those themes when they occur. Sometimes, like archeologists at a dig, we may overlook a shard of pottery or a chip of human bone—the very things that would have led us to Tut's tomb if only we had dug a little deeper.

5. COLLABORATING WITH THEME

Why look for themes *after* you've started writing? Why not begin your novels or stories with themes already in mind? For the same reason most of us don't start our days knowing what lessons or themes will emerge from them. And because the creative unconscious doesn't like to be kept on a leash. Of the forty or so stories I've written, half were drafted with no conscious awareness of what they were about. Instead. I had a clear sense of who the characters were, and what situations they were in, and of the setting in which those situation occurred. Something—I knew (or felt)—lay at the heart of it all, but I didn't know what. Anyway I wasn't sure.

For example, I wrote a story called "The Wolf House," but when I first wrote it I didn't know that this would be its title. The working title was "The Pond," since the bulk of the story took place at a pond where the characters—a group of former high school friends reunited for the funeral of one of their mothers—converge after the wake. By the time I got to the third draft I realized that the pond was not the story's true center; something else was pushing its way out. Since he was a child Andrew, the narrator, one of the reunited friends (and also a twin), has fantasized as many boys do that he was raised not by his parents but by a family of wolves. This fantasy is supported by the legend of Romulus and Remus (taught to him and his brother by their grandmother), and by another myth that had a den of wolves living in the crawlspace under the rotting guest cottage behind his home.

More and more, as I kept revising, this wolf motif attracted me, and so I nudged it along. On an island at the pond's center Andrew and his friends discover mysterious animal droppings. "Wolves," Andrew surmises. I gave the surname "Wolff" to the dead mother and Lenny, her son, and wove in a subplot involving wolf sightings by local residents. And yet I still didn't know why the wolves were important. What did they mean?

Until one day, as I was reworking the final scene, I came across this line of Andrew's in his narration, as he holds his twin brother's hand in the rain at the funeral. "Families are strange things, especially when they're not really families but just odd mixtures of people living under the same roof." The line had always been there, yet only now did its significance strike me. Of course! The story is about the bonds of friendship and family, about how arbitrary and tenuous these can be: how our "closest" relationships, those predicated by blood and circumstance, are weaker than those born of myth and desire. To drive this thematic point home, in the story's ultimate scene Andrew confronts the captured "dangerous" wolf at the dog pound and gets his nose licked.

"The lines of motion that interest the writer are usually invisible," wrote Flannery O'Connor. "They are the lines of spiritual motion. And in this story you should be on the lookout for such things as the action of grace on the Grandmother's soul, and not for the dead bodies." Here O'Connor addresses an audience of readers regarding her best-known story, "A Good Man is Hard to Find," about a middle-class Atlanta family brutally murdered by criminals while on their way to a Florida vacation. By "the lines of motion" O'Connor means theme, or might as well. In a word, the theme of her story is grace, which Merriam-Webster defines as "unmerited divine assistance given man for his regeneration or sanctification" and also as "kindness" and "approval." Read the story and you'll see how the notion of grace attaches itself equally to the criminals and their victims: how everything in O'Connor's story touches, or is touched by, grace.

Are all themes this easy to locate? No. Some can be dug up with a stick; others require a metal detector, or a Geiger counter. One reason why the central theme in a story may remain obscure is because there are too many themes. In her helpful Web site (www.rachelsimon.com), Rachael Simon, author of *Riding the Bus with my Sister,* calls this "thematic greediness," and says that in their eagerness to cram all that they know and think about life into a single story, inexperienced writers invariably overload it with themes. Such eagerness speaks more of impatience and lack of humility than of greed. Anyway, the result is the same: a work without coherence or focus. "Anything," I once heard someone say, "is the enemy of art." Likewise having *anything* or *everything* as a theme is like having no theme at all.

And stories about everything are far harder to write than stories about *something.* By knowing your theme you make your job easier. Questions of structure and tone which were impossible to answer before you grasped your theme suddenly seem not only answerable, but to have obvious answers.

In a story I wrote about a stranger whose sudden presence in a small town raises hopes and suspicions among its citizens, for the life of me I couldn't figure out the man's background. Where was he from? Why had he come to the town? Only when I had dug up my theme, how people project their own needs onto others, did the answer finally come to me. And it was this: that the man *has* no past, none that he can remember. A victim of severe amnesia secondary to herpes encephalitis, he has lost all of his memories, including his memory of *how* he lost his memory. Of course the man doesn't know this, and neither do the townspeople. But now I knew it, and the story, "Tabula Rasa," wrote itself.

Sometimes solutions to technical problems—problems of plot, characterization or tone—come gift-wrapped in newspaper headlines announcing our themes. In *Illumination and Night Glare*, the unfinished autobiography Carson McCullers dictated from her deathbed, she describes how, after years, she solved the problem that stood between her and writing *The Heart is a Lonely Hunter*:

> My working life was almost blighted at the time I was seventeen and for a number of years, by a novel I simply could not understand. I had at least five or six characters who were very clear in my mind. Each of these characters were always talking to the central character. I understood them, but the main character was unfocused, although I knew he was central to the book. Time and again I thought I would just write these characters as short stories, but always I was restrained, because I knew that this mysterious creation was going to be a novel.
>
> Then suddenly, as I was walking up and down the rug in my living room, skipping every other square in the design, and worn out with the problem I had set for myself, the solution all at once came to me. The central character, the silent one,

> had always been called Harry Minowitz, but as I was thinking and pacing, I realized that he was a deaf mute, and that was why the others were always talking to him, and why, of course, he never answered.
>
> This was a real illumination, lighting each of the characters and bringing the whole book into focus. [Straightaway], Harry Minowitz's name was changed to Singer, as the name was more expressive to the new conception, and with this fresh understanding, the book was well begun.

McCullers goes on to describe how, having arrived at this technical solution, the novel's theme became clear to her: "man's revolt against his own inner isolation." Or, applying our one word system, isolation.

McCullers then went on to write a short preface to her as yet unfinished book wherein she waxes philosophical on this theme, elaborating and broadening it ("There is a deep need in man to express himself by creating some unifying principle of God"). Of course, such philosophical insights aren't dispensed baldly in the finished book. They are illuminated by the characters in their situations, illustrated through action, dramatized. "Plot," author Terry Bain tells us, "is a living illustration of theme—theme in motion."

6. THEME VS. PREMISE

> *"You want to send a message, call Western Union."*
> —Sam Goldwyn

Until now we've spoken of stories whose themes are obscure or unknown to us, or that have little or no theme. But can a story have *too much* theme?

It can, I think, when theme oversteps its bounds and moves from general and abstract (the qualities we try to avoid in our descriptions) to pointed and prescriptive. In other words, when it mutates into a message.

Between message and theme there is a middle ground, however, that bears mentioning. That middle ground is known as a *premise*. Premise is theme plus, the plus being a proposition that the story or novel exists to demonstrate. *Jealousy destroys both the jealous lover and the object of his love* is the premise of *Othello*. Premise presumes the outcome of a plot, and in so doing subverts the characters' wills.

To write from a premise is to write with an agenda. It can work, but it can also lead to stories in which the characters become pawns, subservient to the author's aims. It's like when a scientist conducts an experiment to test a theory to which he's already committed: Being tainted with desire, his observations are prejudiced and therefore worthless.

Stories and novels written with agendas often read like parables, or worse, one of those essays we had to write in high school, with a topic sentence stating our premise, and the rest of the paper backing up to the bay like a dumptruck loaded with evidence supporting it. Those essays were dull to write and duller to read.

For a fiction writer, that approach can be worse than dull; it can be deadly. Remember: *No surprise for the writer, no surprise for the reader.* And the writer who front-loads his novel or story with a philosophical, political, social or artistic message is likely not to surprise or delight anyone. At best one ends up with a so-called novel of ideas, at worst with propaganda.

8. PROPAGANDA

On the propaganda end of the scale are novels like Upton Sinclair's *The Jungle,* about the Chicago meatpacking industry—a novel whose chief intent seems to have been to make the reader never want to eat a sausage again. Sinclair, a skillful writer, mounted his broadside in highly readable, dramatic style. But no sooner do you start reading than you know the author's agenda, one that holds no truck with complex characters, not when they run slaughterhouses.

The list of propagandizing novels and stories is long and star-studded, and includes such perennial favorites as Ayn Rand's *Atlas Shrugged*, Shirley Jackson's "The Lottery," and John Steinbeck's *The Grapes of Wrath.* At the risk of arousing the fury of an army of objectivists, I'll start off my discussion with Rand's novel.

Though many would stop short at calling her a philosopher, no one can deny Ayn Rand's power and legitimacy as an author and a thinker. As a novelist she has a lot going for her, too: grand plots, passionate characters, a prose style which—when not driven to foaming rants—is as sweeping and passionate as the plots and characters it conveys. If Ayn Rand writes like someone possessed, it's because she *was* possessed—by the notion that, to truly be men, men must be free, and to be free they must resist the compromises and hypocrisies of any morality based on altruism, while embracing rational self-interest. The information provided to us by our senses is all we need to survive and make moral choices, and the only economic system consistent with such a reality-based morality is laissez-faire capitalism. This is Ayn Rand's philosophy, objectivism, in a nutshell, and as a political philosophy it may have some virtues.

But when you impose such a philosophy on the characters in a work of fiction, problems arise. At best the characters start looking very black and white, like football players on an old, pre-color TV, with the heroic Howard Roarks and Hank Reardons lined up against the sniveling Ben Nealys and Bertram Scudders (note the subtly chosen names). My favorite scene in *Atlas Shrugged*—which, except for John Galt's endless harangue, I read with great if not always intended amusement—is the one where Rand, having loaded a passenger train with sniveling, altruistic, fraudulent wimps, sends it and its coal-burning locomotive into an inadequately (thanks to more sniveling wimps) ventilated tunnel, asphyxiating all. To read such a scene without bursting into laughter requires either great self-control or no sense of humor, but you can't possibly take Rand seriously.

Well, some people can. I see them often on the subway, hunched over one of Rand's thick tomes. In fact my experience suggests that half of the books being read on New York subway trains are *Atlas Shrugged*, the other half are *The Fountainhead.* And the readers are all young women. Why? Because Rand's novels are not only powerful, but empowering, especially to those who feel discriminated against and diminished, as women still do in our culture.

Similar problems are raised by Steinbeck's *The Grapes of Wrath,* a beautifully written but otherwise typical proletariat novel of the decade between the World Wars, a time when authors' and readers' sympathies alike tended to run against the monarchy (read: owners) and in favor of the Bolsheviks (read: tenants and sharecroppers). As Steinbeck never questioned his theme (humanity's struggle in the face of faceless capitalist greed), he likewise never felt the need to turn the landowners in his novel into real people. In service to his message the bad guys remain "faceless," while the Joads, his heroic sharecroppers, are evoked in all their loveable human warmth and complexity.

Am I saying *The Grapes of Wrath* is a bad novel? No, only a worse novel than it might have been had the author's approach to his material been less preordained and heavy-handed. Again, good and even wonderful novels are written with such a heavy hand, like Joseph Heller's *Catch-22*, which takes as its premise that wars are engineered and executed by madmen who drive each other and everyone mad—a premise which, to the book's advantage, is hard to disagree with.

Because its propaganda is both obvious and outrageous, Heller's novel is worth talking about. It is set in a small fictional Italian island during World War II. Its characters are military men associated with a U.S. airbase there. These are the *objects* with which the novel deals. The subject, as stated, is lunacy, specifically the lunacy of war. Did Heller know this before he began writing? I suspect so, given that this theme is so adamantly and redundantly expressed by nearly every scene in the book—to the point (one may argue) of lunacy. This may be yet another argument for *not* knowing our themes too well or too early, as it can lead to stridency or shrillness, if not to downright didacticism.

"A story is not a carrier pigeon with a message clamped to its leg," David Madden admonishes in his good book, *Revising Fiction*. One problem with knowing your theme too early and well is that, like cider left too long in the jug, it may ferment into something much stronger: a premise or, worse, a message. In the case of *Catch-22,* that message is clear and quite vinegary: to survive the lunacy of war you have to be a lunatic. That's *Catch-22* in one sentence, a sentence revisited, with infinite variations, over 472 pages—which, depending on the reader, is either tiresome or hysterical. Still, however one feels about Heller's best novel, no one can deny his conviction in writing it or the brutal pungency of his characters and situations. Propaganda or not, by almost any standard it is a masterpiece.

Lower on the propaganda scale are novels like Camus' *The Plague,* in which he cloaks his message in metaphor, turning the forces of fascism into a plague spread by rats. Thanks to his overarching metaphor, and because Camus is a shrewd and sensitive observer of human nature, the resulting novel feels less didactic than it might. That said, I much prefer *The Stranger,* in which Camus abandons all agendas beyond grappling with the human condition in all its absurdity, with all its injustices. In this novel Camus rises high above the clouds of politics and newspaper headlines to provide us a brutally clear view of an existentially naked man.

9. The Novel of Ideas

Halfway along the continuum, starting with stories whose themes are arrived at purely through wonder and instinct, and ending with those wherein they're preached as propaganda, are stories of which the theme is more of a theory or idea than a message. In such stories the plot is typically a kind of experiment in which the theory is put to the test—

usually with positive results.

In *A Clockwork Orange*, Anthony Burgess' dystopian tale of a London besieged by hooligans, the experiment is carried out on two levels, the novel being level one, while level two consists of the Pavlovian methods of negative reinforcement applied to the novel's head hooligan by scientists intent on "curing" him. The reader reads to learn the results of the experiment[s], and in so doing confronts the question: *Which evil is greater, the loss of free will, or its expression through violence?*

What keeps the novel of ideas from degenerating into pure propaganda is that the question, however clearly stated, is never entirely answered. Though it may uphold the theory, the experiment never *proves* anything. It only presents us with a possibility: in the above case, that the treatment for society's ills may be as bad as or worse than the cure.

In his novel *Lord of the Flies*, William Golding ditches a group of young English schoolboys on a desert island and lets them form their own society. Through his novelistic experiment Golding makes a convincing case for evil as an inherent human trait as opposed to something learned. It's not a pretty theory, or—as messages go—one that any of us wants to hear. But as the experiment is conducted in the tightly sealed test tube of Golding's fictional setting, with no propagandistic finger-wagging at society as a whole, we accept the experiment's results and buy into Golding's theory, at least long enough to *think* about it.

These are grade-A novels of ideas. But such novels come in lower grades and jam bestseller lists. Michael Crichton's *Jurassic Park* is a novel of ideas; so is Dan Brown's *The Da*

Vinci Code. In such books plot and characterization are totally subservient to their authors' preordained ideas: Theme does not follow, but leads. These books may be page turners, yet one doesn't read them for their literary merit or to gain insight into human nature, but to learn about dinosaurs and to decipher chains of cryptic codes.

And even grade-A novels of ideas are bound to be hamstrung and heavy-handed compared with works in which the characters, not their authors, decide their fates. For this reason we search for themes in our work, rather than search for works to go with our themes. A story, after all, is not an instrument for solving life's problems. It is a window or a door, not a fountain of wisdom or an oracle to be consulted in times of strife for truths and answers.

Chekhov put it best. He said, "The writer's task is not to solve the problem but to state the problem correctly."

CHAPTER XIX:
Revision

"Fall seven times, stand up eight."
—Japanese proverb

IX: REVISION

When it comes to writing fiction, there are two types of people in the world: those who revise, and those who don't. Those who don't make up the majority and are amateurs. Having spewed their raw inspirations onto the page, they assume the results to be gold, if not platinum. They've yet to learn that for every sentence sprung fully formed and perfect like Athena from the forehead of Zeus, ten others must be dragged bloody and blue from the womb, resuscitated, and put on ventilators until they can breathe on their own.

Such scribblers assume that, having delivered themselves of their unadulterated genius, it becomes an editor's job to supply such trifles as grammar, punctuation, syntax, logic, structure, and even—in the event of *unmitigated* genius—meaning. And while it's true that the hulking and disheveled Thomas Wolfe plopped a manuscript of equal bulk and sloppiness on editor Maxwell Perkins' desk and saw it published, it's also true that Perkins willingly spent days on end working *mano-a-mano* with Wolfe to shape Wolfe's untidy elephantine opus into a book. But those days—and editors like Perkins—are long gone.

Nowadays, editors hardly have time to edit, let alone

collaborate on, their author's books; they're busy meeting with marketing people, trying to get them to publish those books in the first place. As hard as you work to sell your novel or story to an editor, she must work as hard to sell it to her publisher. Darken her desk with a messy manuscript and (as we editors like to say) it will get read *very* quickly.

Does that mean editors *never* edit? No; they do, and my guess is it's their favorite part of the job. But given the choice between a manuscript that's near perfect and one needing oodles of work, guess which one they'll go to bat for?

And unlike Lana Turner, who (contrary to legend) was discovered not by a movie producer at Schwabb's Pharmacy, but by a newspaper editor while drinking soda at the Top Hat Café, you can't rely on the kindness of strangers to rescue you or your prose from oblivion.

So—you should revise.

1. Revision vs. Rewriting: What's the Difference?

Often I am asked by students to distinguish between rewriting and revision. According to my Webster's they mean exactly the same thing. Revise: "To look over again in order to correct or improve." Rewrite: "To revise something previously written." Yet grounds exist for confusion. When an editor asks me to revise something that I've written, the word "revise" feels warm and encouraging against my skin—like a coach's friendly pat on the back as he sends me back out into the playing field. When the same editor says "rewrite," it chills me to the bone, and I feel that I have failed in some fundamental way, that I must throw out everything and start all over again.

I suppose there are times when revision isn't enough, when we must begin from scratch and forget all that we have done before—or find another editor to look at our work. But for the purpose of this chapter we'll assume your early drafts are worth going the distance for. If you think so, then they probably are.

2. WHEN TO REVISE

Those white-hot bursts of creative fervor (supplemented by gallons of black coffee) that blew you through your first draft won't do for the revision process, which requires a cooler, calmer, less-caffeinated head. Wordsworth defined poetry well as "emotion *recollected in tranquility.*" The italics are mine, and emphasize the need to apply objectivity and prudence to what starts out as inspiration and emotion; i.e., the revision process. The cartoony image of a poet being seized epileptic-like by inspiration and flinging his masterpiece—along with buckets of spit and sweat—onto the page, is about as realistic as Wile E. Coyote's expectation of catching the Road Runner with a giant magnet and rocket-propelled roller skates. Real poets work calmly at their desks and spend days if not weeks or months revising a poem of a few dozen lines, working through draft after draft after draft.

You needn't go that far, or as far as Oscar Wilde, who complained to his diary once that, having spent a morning putting a comma into one of his stories, he spent the afternoon "taking it out." There is the danger, as Lawrence Durrell warns, of fussing (Durrell used a stronger verb) with things too much.

Still—and though you may not be a poet—you can and

should be a stylist, meaning you should be every bit as dedicated to language, to choosing and arranging your words.

First, though, you need to get into the right emotional state for editing; you need to cool down, put some objective distance between yourself and what you've written. How?

There are several ways, the ideal and most obvious being to literally distance yourself by going away or doing something else for a while. Let your words, and you with them, chill. The more time you spend staring at your own sentences, the more they calcify in the mind, to where changing a word feels like chipping away at solid marble.

Time soaks the words, softening them, and is therefore considered by many, myself included, the best of all editors. A year from now—even a month or three weeks from now—look at the draft of your story or novel and I bet you'll see room for improvement. Meanwhile write something else, or take a vacation (I recommend one of the less popular Greek islands).

Unfortunately we writers don't always have the luxury of time. Deadlines must be met, and/or we have nothing else to work on. That being so, you should still let *some* time go by, as revising in a hurry has its perils, as Virginia Woolf discovered when revising *The Voyage Out*:

> When I read the thing over (one very gray evening) I thought it so flat and monotonous that I did not even 'feel' the 'atmosphere': certainly there was no character in it. Next morning I proceeded to slash and rewrite, in the hope of animating it, and (as I suspect for I have not re-

read it) destroying the one virtue it had–a kind of
continuity; for I wrote it originally in a dream-like
state, which was at any rate, unbroken. … I have
kept all the pages I cut out, so the thing can be
reconstructed precisely as it was.

Woolf makes a good case for saving all drafts. Then
again had she waited a bit longer before revising she might
not have thrown out the Wedgewood with the dishwater.

While some writers can get away with writing in the
morning, breaking for lunch, and revising all afternoon,
others (like Woolf) clearly need to wait longer. Whatever
you do, don't revise while still in a state of creative agita-
tion or ecstasy, or when feeling depressed, exhausted, de-
spondent, bitter, or filled with self-loathing. Remember the
scarlet Kerouac baseball cap my writer friend dons when
drafting? Before revising, make sure you've replaced it with
your Zen Buddhist editor's cap.

Other ways to enhance editorial objectivity: Read your
words out loud to yourself. Sit down somewhere, manuscript in one hand and pencil in the other, and read as if
to a crowded room. As you read, note things that bother
you, imprecise words and faulty rhythms, mixed or forced
metaphors, dim descriptions, anything that befogs or puts
a bump in the narrative road. Note especially those places
where you feel your eyes glazing over (and if your first drafts
are anything like mine, you will).

If reading to yourself feels as lonely as a lost shoe, find
someone else to read your first drafts to (believe it or not,
such people exist who haven't been beatified). Sit her down
in front of you and do as above, still with pencil in hand

[223]

and stopping to make notes, but with a live body listening. Even without laughter or applause a live audience tells you a lot about your work. You can feel a lisener's interest wax and wane. If she wishes to comment afterwards, let her. By then, though, chances are you'll already know what needs doing.

The following solution for gaining distance from your words may sound weird, but it works: Print your draft out in an unusual (but not illegible) font and in a different format (with wider margins, for instance). You may not recognize your own words. This will help you see them with fresh eyes.

If you've done all of the above and feel you need more help, get feedback from others. Here, a good writing workshop may help, or better still a fellow writer whose aesthetics are a good match for yours. Whoever criticizes your work (contrary to a common misconception, the verb *to criticize* covers both positive remarks and, um, suggestions for improvement) should sympathize with your intentions. (If she doesn't like what you're trying to do, she has no business telling you how to do it.)

Last resort: Work with a professional editor. There are plenty out there, drawn from the swollen ranks of writers looking for a bit of extra income. For a price they will gladly give you feedback, and odds are it will be useful.

That said, no editor's advice should be followed slavishly. It's your work: You've got to know when to take suggestions and when to say no thanks. Sometimes an editor's efforts will tighten and clean up your prose when you want it rumpled and filthy. Know that editors tend to err on the side of conservatism. As Tennessee Williams once lamented to Gore Vidal after Vidal had line-edited one of Williams' more eccentric stories, "You have corrected all of my faults, and they are all that I have!"

Should you, in seeking feedback from others, meet with comments not only unhelpful, but discouraging or destructive, bear in mind these immortal words:

> *"A book is a mirror. If an ass peers into it,*
> *you can't expect an apostle to look out."*
> —G. C. Lichtenberg

3. WHAT TO REVISE

> *"Don't f--- with it too much."*
> —Lawrence Durrell

On one side of the equation we have Mr. Durrell advocating a light touch, on the other Don Newlove commanding, "Revise till your fingers bleed!" Top brass dispensing irreconcilable orders. Whose advice so follow?

I say follow both sets of marching orders, with this proviso: operating on yourself isn't easy. When first performing open-heart surgery on your prose you're sure to botch a procedure or two, and will as surely lose some patients as you learn to distinguish between living and dead tissue. There's no way around this bloody mess except to keep your first drafts; in the event of a super hatchet job you can always go back to the original (real doctors can't do this). Better to butcher your prose than to risk never learning to edit at all.

Suggestion: Having finished your first draft, start over. Open a brand new document on your computer and, referring to your draft only occasionally, retype your whole story or novel, rethinking every moment, every sentence. Duplicate your draft only when it's worth duplicating, when you can't possibly improve it.

Or write from scratch, never referring to the other versions, as D. H. Lawrence did three times with *Lady Chatterly's Lover,* producing three different novels on the same subject. Old words can block fresh insights. Like Lawrence, I once rewrote a novel purely from memory, remembering only what was worthy in the original, forgetting the rest. Songwriters work this way, carrying tunes inside their heads and not on paper. The catchy tunes incubate while the weak ones dissolve, edited by memory.

Two drafts may be all, or just the beginning. It's not unheard of for a writer to go through five or ten drafts, or more, on a single story or chapter. I've done it. And ten drafts later some stories still molder in a file drawer. Does that make me a fool? No, because after twenty drafts they may yet be published, and published well.

On the other hand I've had stories published that took only two drafts. Some stories are easier to write then others. But the hard ones are as worth writing.

Raymond Carver, one of this country's best short fiction writers, owned up to revising his stories on average no fewer than a dozen times—with Gordon Lish's help, according to some (including Gordon Lish). Whoever helped him, however much help he got, Carver understood well that real writers revise.

4. BIG STUFF

If a first draft is the place to write from the heart, free of self-judgment and other forms of doubt and worry, subsequent drafts are the place to worry over everything, and heed all the sage advice on craft to be found in this and other books. "No sentimentality about this job," Daphne du Maurier tells us of the editor's task. You may choose to devote a whole draft to a single element of craft, going through scene by scene improving dialogue, then spend the next draft coalescing theme.

Whatever your approach, before addressing little things (like whether to use dashes or parentheses), make sure that the Big Things are in order.

Some Big Things to consider:

Characters. Ask yourself: Do I have all the characters I need to tell my tale? Are characters sufficiently motivated? Can I afford to lose a few? Have I written stereotypes? Are any of my main characters too flat? Do they fulfill their roles too neatly?

Plotting and pacing. What's the first interesting thing that happens in my story, and how far is it from where the story actually begins? Does my story or novel raise a question that is answered by the plot, but only when it reaches its climax and not before? Have I taken full advantage of the tension leading up to that climax? Have I judiciously selected scenes? Is my ending both surprising *and* inevitable (or if not inevitable, at least plausible)?

Point of view and tense. Have I chosen the best possible point or points of view? Should I stick to one character's viewpoint, or alternate between points of view? Does my use of the present tense rob the narrative of perspective, and flatten the story arc, or add drama and immediacy?

Dialogue. Is my dialogue speakable? Is it *too* real, as if

[227]

transcribed from a tape-recorder? Have I overused stage directions? Are there too many attributions (dialogue tags), or too few? Do my characters mouth too many banalities and clichés? Are lines burdened with forced exposition? Does the dialogue evoke character and, more importantly, does it entertain?

Description and setting. Have I neglected to embody my characters, to give them limbs, clothing, faces, gestures? And what about my scenes? Do they take place in a void? Have I emphasized one sense at the expense or exclusion of all the others? Have I made the most of my setting, descriptively and metaphorically? What about weather and atmosphere? Are some of my descriptions too lush, or too long? Do they digress? Or are they too meager, too thin?

Flashbacks. First, are my flashbacks necessary and, if so, are they properly motivated? Should I rearrange my material to get rid of the clumsy flashback in the middle of that love scene? Is a flashback too long? Does it detach us from the main story?

Voice and style. Does my chosen voice suit the material? Should my tone be more or less formal? Is the narrator's diction consistent?

Themes and motifs. Recall Flannery O'Conner's "I write because I don't know what I think until I read what I say." At best, theme is a result, not a cause. Likewise motifs emerge naturally and spontaneously as we write, or ought to. When they do, though, as authors we're responsible for recognizing and underscoring them. Remember the green light at the end of Daisy's dock, and then ask yourself: Have I woven subtle threads of motif and theme subtly yet thoroughly throughout my story or novel?

5. LITTLE STUFF

The devil being, as they say, in the details, we should pay close attention to the little things. Here are some:

Grammar and punctuation. Grammar is a convention, something civilized people can agree upon. To the extent that conventions are rules, creative souls are free to break them, but only for a good reason. In writing this sentence, I spell the words according to Webster's dictionary, pause with a comma after the dependent clause ending in the word *sentence,* capitalize the first word and end with a period. But what if i chooz not to dew so what if i chooz to dispenss with speling an punkchewayshun an yooz ownlee lowurkaze ledderz My guess is you'll be confused, if not infuriated.

Grammar is one of the few things—maybe the only thing—that keeps writers civilized. Use it. Not slavishly or mindlessly, but with due respect for the considerable minds that have brought it to bear over ages. An indented paragraph is a lovely thing: Why so many choose to dispense with indents is beyond me. Punctuation marks are dramatic personae: the ebullient exclamation mark, the impulsive dash, the coy ellipse, the intellectual semi-colon. According to at least one legend, a simple comma, improperly placed, can save a life. During the nineteenth century, captured Irish rebels were typically hanged, the alternative being exile to a place called Van Dieman's Land, known to us as Tasmania. The legend maintains that a woman once inadvertently spared a handsome rebel from being exiled by transposing a comma in the order signed by her lieutenant husband, who had written, "Pardon impossible, to be sent to Van Dieman's Land." She changed it to read, "Pardon, impossible to be sent to Van Dieman's Land." In both cases a semicolon would have been more appropriate, but let us not quibble. The point is, punctuation matters.

Be inventive by all means, but why reinvent the wheel and throw out hundreds of years of perfected convention? Better to pour those energies into creating memorable characters, exciting scenes, vivid descriptions. For every reader you gain by breaking a convention, you are likely to lose a dozen. Kerouac's claims for spontaneous prose notwithstanding, his one commercially successful novel, *On the Road*, obtained its final paragraphed and punctuated form from Malcolm Cowley—his editor at Viking. Though Cowley's efforts earned him an ungrateful author's endless scorn, they also secured Kerouac's enduring fame.

But this is no place for a grammar lesson; a good book on English usage can give you that. Also, if you haven't done so already, buy a copy of *The Element's of Style*, by William Strunk Jr. and E.B. White. This modestly slim volume takes up no more space than T.S. Eliot's poem *The Waste Land*, and it's as good. What you need to know (and more) about the uses and abuses of the English language is in there, and more, including such disarming advice as "Be clear."

Not that you should sell your artistic soul to Strunk & White, or to anyone else. But before breaking conventions, know them, at least. Only once mastered can they be broken with flair. Otherwise, people may just think you're dumb.

"To be or not to be"—*not* to be. The words *is*, *was*, and *were* are all variants of the verb *to be*, which, among lifeless verbs, wears the heavyweight crown. While most verbs are chosen for their evocative or kinetic powers, *to be* paints no picture in the mind, conveys no action, makes no dent in the reader's psyche. It says practically nothing. To find a deader word, you'd have to reach for an article or a conjunction, for *the* or *and*.

Which begs the question: Why do so many writers lean on the progressive tense? Why write, "Sam *was wearing* red socks," when you can write, "Sam *wore* red socks?" Why, "Susan *is running,"* when she *runs* will get her there faster?

True, in conversation people tend to speak this way. It sounds friendlier, softer. Which explains why, in the merry, merry month of May, I didn't *walk* down the street one day; I *was walking*. The progressive has its place, not just in corny old songs, but when someone performs a progressive act ("Rover *was* busy *digging* up the back yard)." But used too frequently, or out of lazy habit, like a carnivorous wasp it sucks the meat out of otherwise healthy prose. That space taken up by *is* or *was* might have held a strong, active verb. "A lamp *was standing* on the end table." Okay. "A lamp *stood* on the end table." Better.

Metaphors. Are my metaphors fresh, organic, and necessary? Do they help the reader? Have I used a simile where a metaphor would be stronger? Have I stumbled on a cliché?

Clichés. "His green eyes shined twin beams of light and there was magic in the air between them." Clichés are like those little crosses you see at the sides of highways: They mark a place where a genuine feeling or insight has met its doom. When, reading over your draft, your eyes come across a familiar-sounding moment or group of words, odds

[231]

are you've come upon such a disaster area. And it needn't be something as obvious as the above, or as that crown jewel of clichés, "It's raining cats and dogs." "Heart of stone" is a cliché; so is whatever moves "like greased lightning." Many clichés are innocuous. "Scared to death" qualifies; so do "cut to the chase," "sweating profusely," and "grinding poverty." Reading clichés is like chewing air. But recycled often enough, even "the heaventree of stars hung with humid nightblue fruit"—the most striking line in *Ulysses*—risks turning into a cliché.

Modifiers. Nothing wrong with adverbs and adjectives —as long as they pull more than their own weight by being fresh, unpredictable. Above all they must add something that isn't obvious or trite to the words they modify.

Attributive phrases. Remember *said,* that "most watery of words"? Don't be afraid to use it as often as you want to. Ask yourself: Are those speaking my dialogue clearly identified? Do I need to insert an extra attribution here and there? Can I cut a few? Are my stage directions intrusive or unnecessary—or both?

Excommunicate Latinisms. A Latinism is a bulky word derived from the Latin. Too often writers tend to use them where a simple, plain, Anglo-Saxon equivalent would do. For instance, don't have people converse when they can talk. If Hank goes to the package store, he can buy a bottle of Rock & Rye, he needn't purchase it. Assuming that they belong anywhere, words like *variegated, ascertain, beneficial, extrapolate, resumption, extemporaneous,* and *preliminary* belong in corporate quarterly reports, legal briefs, and sociological studies, and not—unless the fiction aims to replicate the tone of such things—in good fiction..

Why is so much professional writing bad? Because it's pretentious; because it imitates clear, concise writing while being neither clear nor concise. People say lawyers write badly. But legal writing, done well, can be gorgeous (see Judge M. Woolsey's ruling on *Ulysses*). Bad legal writing isn't bad because it's legal, but because it's bad. To paraphrase Tolstoy, all bad writing is bad in pretty much the same ways, pretentiousness being the worst of them.

The easiest way to be pretentious is to use pretentious words, words like *ascertain* and *perpetrate*. "At this point in time we have ascertained that the perpetrator has been apprehended." ... At this point in time I'd like you to forget forever the phrase *at this point in time*. Do it *now*. Likewise forget *the fact that*, *the question whether*, and *the majority of.* Bury *basically:* put it (to skirt a cliché) where the sun don't percolate. Lose *literally*. *Seemingly* sucks; so do most adverbs with three or more syllables. Beware of words ending in *-tion*. Ditto *ism, acy, ance, ness*, and *ment*. Such words are for politicians, not poets, and for a few pretentious narrators like Nabokov's Humbert, who'd be lost without his lexicon.

When in doubt, cross out or replace the overripe words and simplify. Your readers will extend gratitude to thank you.

Journalese. Writing *ohne Salz und Schmalz*—without salt or fat—is worth reading once, if that. Shake some salt and pepper into it, lay in some nice, buttery metaphors. Or make your prose lean and clean so it goes down like broth. Don't settle for language as mere information.

Now let's look at big and small things together and read the first paragraphs of a draft story.

6. REVISING "WOUND"

In the chapter on theme I discussed a story by one of my workshop participants in which a young woman confronts her emergent sexuality during a weekend visit by an old friend of her clock-collecting father. Originally, and for reasons unclear even to her, Lisa Kunick titled her story "Sweet Onion." By draft two the title had changed to "Wound."

Here is how "Wound" opens:

> A man named Rick stayed with my father and me
> when I started high school. My father introduced
> him as an old friend from the Comic Book club
> at Hamilton High, the same school that I had
> attended for two years.

Before discussing this opening paragraph, I want to say a few words about the new title, which improves on the old one by being much more thematically relevant. A young woman's sexuality is certainly an open wound of a sort, a source of vulnerability and potential injury and pain, but also open in the way that curiosity opens us to discoveries and danger. And any man knows too well that a woman's sexuality can itself wound. For all we know the title may have a double or ironic meaning, pointing toward dad's friend, Rick, as the possible object of some injury.

That said, the title may be too stated and diffuse. How many stories can you think of where the title "Wound" might apply? If the answer is "too many," then that's a good reason to find a more specific title. Also, unless used ironically, "Wound" pleads too much sympathy for the main character. And since readers can't presume—let alone be certain of—any such ironic intention, they're likely to take the title literally at least to begin with, and sigh, thinking they're in for a "victim story."

While the search for a perfect title continues, let's turn to the first paragraph, which has one very good thing going for it: It gets the story off to a running start with a declaration of the inciting incident, the thing that sets the story in motion, Rick's arrival. Still, the sentence could be much more specific, and loaded properly so that the important information comes—like the punchline of a joke—at the end. Also, since this is a story about an adolescent told from the perspective of her older self looking back, we need some clue to this, a date being the obvious solution. Lastly, as written, the paragraph implies that the narrator is about to start attending the same high school she "had attended for two years." Unless, like Billy Pilgrim in *Slaughterhouse-Five*, the narrator has become unstuck in time, that needs clearing up.

Here's Lisa's revised opening:

> The summer of 1991—the summer before I was to begin my sophomore year at Hamilton High— my father, an estate lawyer and collector of antique watches and clocks, invited an old friend of his to spend the weekend with us.

In this version we lose the name of the father's friend (which can come later when he and the narrator are introduced) and the fact that he and the father went to the same high school together. What's gained is a sense of who the father is, through his vocation and his hobby. Now we know the story looks back through time. And two bland sentences have been replaced by a single, stronger one in which the narrator's voice trips (rather endearingly, I would say) over its own feet in supplying to us that key piece of information: that she was soon to start high school, i.e., that she was fourteen years old. That stuttered aside is really what the entire story turns on, and its tossed-off quality makes it all the more moving.

Let's examine two more paragraphs of this same story:

"My daughter, Becky," my father said, extending one arm up the banister as if announcing my debutante debut. When he looked up the stairs, he frowned. I had just stepped out of the shower when the doorbell rang, and had dressed quickly in jeans and a sweatshirt two sizes too big that said UCLA across the chest, my father's alma mater.

"Like father like daughter," Rick said as I reached the bottom step and shyly extended my hand. I assumed he referred to something he saw in my face, perhaps my pronounced nose or my heart shaped jaw. He shook my hand vigorously and too long, as though I might miss the handshake if he abated. Rick, who seemed wider than he was tall, smelled of anise and spoke softly for a man his size. I leaned in to hear what he said, bestowing importance to his every word. The brightly colored plaids of his shirt and shorts suggested whim and possibly golf. A helmet sat on the chair next to the door. I looked down at his tasseled

loafers, the only sign that this man and my father
could possibly be friends.

From the opening paragraph (now reduced to an opening sentence) we know this meeting is to have consequences—perhaps dire, perhaps not; but anyway, it sits at the center of the story. So it deserves to be dramatized. But in the
first sentence above, dad's introduction drops from the sky,
disembodied, with the narrator (Becky) similarly reduced to
a pair of ears. Two sentences later we learn that she has just
showered and dressed. Where is Becky now? Presumably at
the top of the stairs, where Rick's frowning eyes have found
her. As presented the scene is so blurry it hardly comes across
as a scene at all. What this movie needs is a director, someone to tell the cameraman where to focus, so that a scene is
painted wherein the narrator, freshly showered and spruced,
sees this male stranger looking up at her from the vestibule
below. Since we're clearly meant to identify with the narrator
of this tale, to share her viewpoint, the camera should frame
what *she* sees, as she sees it, and (perhaps) zoom in for a
description of the strange man's frowning eyes. Thus we see
him, too—a subjective view, to be sure, but far better than
none at all. Then—as Becky tucks in her sweatshirt (a gesture which, in its proper place, may signify her nervousness,
vanity, or both) dad makes his introductory remark.

In its present form, the reader inhabits the circumstances of this scene only in retrospect, assembling them like a
jigsaw puzzle after the fact, when it could have come pre-
assembled. Properly constructing this moment would also
slow the scene down, increasing tension, instead of letting

it all happen biff-bang-boom—or rather boom-bang-biff, as things are a bit scrambled here. By the time we get to Rick's trite opener—a line that dispels any hope that he might be charming—we should be properly set up for the disappointment. Or maybe—to mitigate the damage that such a line would likely inflict on a Becky's budding sexual curiosity—Rick delivers it "with a quick smile and a nod of his stubbled, square jaw"—something to pull it (and him) back from the brink and keep the reader wondering: Is Rick a prince, or a clod?

Sounds nitpicking? It is—but it's just the sort of nitpicking you need to do when revising your own stories, interrogating every sentence, asking, "Is the focus right here? Am I painting a clear enough picture? Am I fully exploiting the point of view and creating tension?" In drafting stories you try to inhabit your characters; you put yourself in their shoes. In revising them, put yourself in the reader's shoes.

A few lines later we get to the handshake—their first touch—another loaded moment in what we already know is a story of sexual awakening. "He shook my hand vigorously and too long, as though I might miss the handshake if he stopped." Yes, or as though *he'd* miss it. The innocent narcissism of this last observation is belied both by the fact that the narrator is looking back over time and by the following line ("Rick, who seemed wider than he was tall, smelled of anise and spoke softly for a man of his size"), which makes the same narrator sound more than a little mature, as if she's dated (and inhaled) men of all shapes and sizes. This incongruity needs to be addressed: The narrator can't be fourteen and thirty at the same time. Stories like this one, where a narrator looks back in time, are a balancing act; you need to know when to introduce the older perspective, and when to stay in the moment and mind of the younger person whose story the reader is following. Generally, when dramatizing a scene, stay in the moment, and leave hindsight interpretations to the reader when not introducing them *between* dramatic scenes.

We're still only halfway through the first page. And though I seem to be dishing up lots of criticism, I chose Lisa's story not for its flaws, but because her first draft was so strong. All the working parts were there, they just need to be assembled more precisely, and recalibrated and elaborated on in places.

Do all these questions and concerns make revision seem arduous, if not impossible? Remember that when growing a story—and that's what we're doing here—you need to see every moment as a seed, every sentence as an opportunity to make something better, richer, deeper, clearer. Novices talk about revision as though it were torture. But for experienced writers this is where the fun comes in, this chance to turn a draft horse (so to speak) into a Thoroughbred.

Let's leave off our interrogation of this first draft on a positive note. The next three sentences, starting with "I leaned in to hear what he said …" plant us perfectly in Becky's viewpoint, while making it implicit that, whatever she may think of this man, she can't keep her thoughts from him. More might be made of that helmet (Is it silver? Gold? Shaped like something meant for outer space? Or one of those black fiberglass coalscuttles favored by the Hells Angels?). And I questioned whether anyone with an interest in survival would ride a motorcycle in street clothes, and, if so, would he wear a helmet? But these really are nitpicks.

Going through her entire story at this level of detail, working on a virgin screen, revising sentence by sentence, Lisa produced a second draft that needed only a quick polish to be worthy of submission.

> The summer of 1991—the summer before I was to begin my sophomore year at Hamilton High—my father, an estate lawyer and collector of antique watches and clocks, invited a childhood friend of his to spend the weekend during a heat wave.
>
> I'd just stepped out of the shower when I heard the doorbell ring, and yanked my favorite jeans—the ones with the bandana patches across both knees—over still steamy legs, and threw on an oversized sweatshirt, the one with UCLA silk-screened across the chest, my dad's alma mater. They were the first things I grabbed out of duffel bag I'd brought for the weekend. I was still trying decide whether to wear my hair loose or tie it back when I heard my father's voice calling to me from the vestibule.
>
> I darted out of the room past the grandfather clock—or the father clock, as I called it. When I reached the top of the stairs I expected to see a man who looked like my father, his identical twin, a man of precision and preparation, the kind who even on weekends at home wore his comb-over impeccably hair-sprayed into place, with slacks pleated as sharp as razor blades. Instead I saw a man who looked like he'd just walked off the set of

a sitcom on which he played Ralph Kramden's contemporary equivalent: the ne'er-do-well slob with a heart of gold. He wore a plaid shirt that looked like he'd worn it still damp and rumpled from the washing machine, and khaki shorts as wrinkled as brown paper bags. He stood with both arms, each as thick as a drainpipe and furry with black hair, resting on the hips of his beefy frame. A shiny red globe-like thing dangled from one of his hands.

"My daughter, Becky," he said, pointing at me up the banister. "Becky, meet Rick. Rick was president of the comic book club back at H.H. when he and I went there. I wanted to be president, but he beat me to the punch. Right, Rick?"

"Right," said Rick, leering at me—at least, it looked leer-like to me. His face was as heavy and wide as the rest of him, with a shovel-like jaw coated with dark stubble and a head of black hair as gnarly and unappetizing as a kitchen mop. Dad, standing with his arm around him as if posing for a picture that no one would take, looked up the stairs at me. Seeing what must have been the less than approving look on my face, he frowned.

"Well—can't you at least say hello?"

"Hi," I said.

"Hey, there," said Rick, putting the globe-like thing, which looked like it had been dispensed by a gigantic gumball machine and which I guessed was a motorcycle helmet, on the stiff-backed vestibule chair where he'd already tossed his leather jacket.

"What are you standing there for?" said my father. "Come down here; don't be shy. He's not

[241]

going to bite you, are you, Rick?"

"I hadn't considered it," said Rick as I made my way shyly down the stairs. "Boy, I'll be damned if she doesn't look like you. Like father, like daughter, as they say," Rick said, nodding as I reached the bottom step and put out my hand. I never thought I looked at all like my father, and didn't take his remark as a compliment, assuming it referred to my pronounced nose or my heart-shaped jaw, the features I most disliked in myself. He shook my hand hard and too long, I thought, as if he didn't want to stop. His fingers felt warm and gooey.

"Well, look at that," he said, still shaking me. "Why you've got yourself a grown woman here, Clarence, practically."

His breath smelled of something like licorice, but less sweet. Black, damp curls sprung up from the back of his neck under his shirt collar, where the helmet had pressed against them; they looked like fiddlehead ferns. I leaned close to hear every word he was saying, clinging to every crass syllable, but he only asked my father whether it was all right for him to park in the street. He kept smiling at me, that leer or a smile, as I glanced shyly down his hairy legs, at the incompatible tasseled loafers he wore—the only sign that he and my father could possibly ever have been friends.

In revising, Lisa has taken the trouble to immerse herself—and us along with her—deeply into the events of her story. We are there, in Becky's shoes, inhabiting her world as she inhabits it. Fiction, at its best, doesn't tell us, or even show us, how other people live. It lets us do their living for ourselves.

Not to describe experiences, but to *create* them: That's the fiction writer's calling.

7. CUTTING & TWEAKING

"Don't scrape, cut."
—Donald Newlove

When we revise, we don't just work with or within our already written words. Unlike oil paints, words cost nothing: use as many as you like, scrape them all away, use some more—no charge. There's no excuse, in other words, for saving your words.

"Omit needless words," say Strunk & White. I couldn't have said it better. For sure I couldn't say it more succinctly.

So much cutting may seem masochistic, but a piece of writing that works well in 5,000 words shouldn't run to 10,000. And you'll be surprised what you can cut. So much that we state is implied; so much that we spell out can be deduced or imagined. Readers want to participate in the story. Do all their imagining for them and they feel left out. And the reader's imagination is a better writer than you or I will ever be. Why not let it do some of the work? What we cut no one but ourselves will ever miss.

"An author is one who can judge his own stuff's worth, without pity, and destroy most of it."
—Colette

Tweaking means crafting sentences and paragraphs, re-orchestrating them, shifting and substituting words until things are as clear, pungent and crisp as possible. Like nip-

[243]

ping and tucking, cutting and tweaking go hand-in-hand.

Compare two versions of the same paragraph by Samantha, a former student of mine. Originally Samantha wrote:

> Traffic whooshed past me, splattering my legs and
> feet with muddy water. I still hadn't worked out
> the criteria that marks a taxi "For Hire" so I treated
> them all as potential kills. I knew it had some-
> thing to do with the small white sign on the top of
> the cab and whether it was lit or not but I hadn't
> noticed a distinct pattern yet. I'd began to doubt
> that there was one. I edged a bit further out onto
> the road peering towards the oncoming traffic.
> The traffic had stopped, stuck behind the traffic
> signals. I couldn't see any taxis, just shiny streets
> reflecting the headlights and the street lights of
> Fifth and Broadway; oh, and rain of course—lots
> of rain, puddles, umbrellas, people running and
> other things associated with rain. As the traffic
> lights changed up the avenue, a new influx of
> traffic surged towards me and I stretched my hand
> even harder to the sky like an eight-year-old who
> knows the answer and is determined to catch her
> teacher's attention. Please, pick me, pleeeeease.
> Here, I'm here, over here. Please.

Not bad, but the moment doesn't justify so many words. The reader's eye gets bogged in all that ink, yearns to skip. Samantha cut and tweaked to this:

> Traffic whooshed by, splattering my legs with gray
> water. I hadn't worked out the lighting system that

> marks a cab "for hire," and so I treated every yel-
> low vehicle as a potential savior. Suddenly the traf-
> fic jammed behind a red light. I saw no more taxis,
> just shiny streets reflecting head and taillights, and
> rain –lots of rain. When the light changed a sea
> of cars and trucks surged toward me. I stretched
> my arm eagerly into the dark wet sky–like a fourth
> former trying to get the teacher's attention.

In the second version the description moves at a pace with the story, which has more important things to do than pelt us with taxis and rain.

Tweaking may be less painful than cutting, but it's trick- ier. It calls for a keen eye and a steady hand and great atten- tion to detail. For every paragraph I've improved through tweaking, I've murdered and mutilated dozens.

Let me share with you, if I may, the evolution of a trou- blesome paragraph from my own novel, *Life Goes to the Mov- ies*. The scene: a restaurant floating on the East River. In the book's earliest draft the scene is merely sketched, with no attempt to evoke mood or atmosphere. It's barely written.

> The wedding took place in August of 1985 on
> a barge on the East River, Brooklyn side. As if
> to celebrate the occasion the stars were out. A
> twelve-piece jazz orchestra played.

Journalese. Now strap yourselves into a time machine and skip ahead a draft or two:

> The wedding reception took place on a barge on
> the East River, with the Brooklyn Bridge humming

> its harpsong in the warm damp air high above
> us. Across the water, Manhattan's rhinestone tiara
> glittered. Carved ice statues cradled sterling caviar
> buckets, while a twelve-piece swing orchestra in
> vanilla jackets and gold derbies bounced brass
> noodles and spun ribbons of silver into the breezy
> dark night.

All those modifiers! Here the author—myself—reaches for Fitzgeraldian lushness and falls on his face. That rhinestone tiara is a dimestore cliché unfit for pulp. Then comes the adjectival parade—*carved, sterling, vanilla, gold, brass, silver, breezy, dark*—one that leaves this reader lurching for a private barge rail from which to throw up. All those brass noodles and silver ribbons are a valiantly misguided attempt at synesthesia, to turn notes for the ear into images for the eye. But the metaphor strays too far from its subject and has me groping for the common denominator between music and noodles.

Glide your time machine forward six months, through two more drafts:

> A canvas-tented barge docked on the Brooklyn
> side of the East River. Summer drizzle softens the
> mucky air as the fabled bridge rasps with car traf-
> fic overhead. Ice mermaids cradle silver buckets
> of caviar, oysters on cracked ice squirm in ragged
> shells; shrimp cling for dear life above flaming
> seas of cocktail sauce. A swing orchestra in vanil-
> la jackets and paper derbies weaves and thumps
> rhythms into the drizzling dark. Across the river,
> meanwhile, the Manhattan skyline wastes as

much electricity as possible.

Better, but still too heavy on the modifiers. Here cutting comes to the rescue, as it almost always does.

Montage, night:
A canvas-tented barge on the East River, Brooklyn side. Drizzle softens the night air as the bridge hums with traffic overhead. Ice mermaids cradle caviar buckets; oysters in cracked shells float on seas of chipped ice; shrimp cling for life over craters of cocktail sauce; a swing band swishes and whumps rhythms into the drizzly dark. Across the dark river, meanwhile, Manhattan wastes as much electricity as possible.

The brass noodles and silver ribbons have been swept off the dance floor, replaced by clinging shrimp and whumping rhythms (the neologism, I think, is earned, since no more suitable verb is to be found in the dictionary). To keep with the novel's theme of life blending with the movies I worked in the screenplay lingo.

Here the emphasis isn't on modifiers but on verbs: *tented, softens, hums, cradle, float, squirm, cling, swishes, whumps*. In retrospect "wastes as much electricity as possible" strikes me as passive, weak, but I could think of no active way of expressing the thought. Maybe you can.

That's how the passage stands. You may take issue with some of my choices. As the Italians say, *Cada uno con su gusto.* Translation: Let each man fall victim to his own tastes.

Not every paragraph involves such struggle. But the troublesome ones are worth the trouble. G.K. Chesterton, one of a dozen authors to whom the dictum "Murder your darlings" is attributed (along with an ecclectic gathering that includes Oscar Wilde, F. Scott Fitzgerald, Samuel Johnson, George Orwell, Dorothy Parker and William Faulkner) is also famous for having said, "If a thing is worth doing, it's worth doing badly."[1]

Needless to say he was talking about writing first drafts, not later ones.

8. The Law of Diminishing Returns: When to Let Go

Revisionitis: the inability of authors to part with their work, the compulsion to go on nipping and tucking until they themselves have been tucked into their graves. Tales of publishers, fed up with missed deadlines, prying manuscripts from their author's clutching hands are as common as authors themselves. Tolstoy's wife recopied *War and Peace* by hand between four and twelve times (depending on which source you trust) for her husband before his publisher pried it from *her* fingers.

The underlying cause of the disease is obvious. Finishing something means accepting its imperfections and limitations, and facing the possibilities of rejection, criticism, and (should you see it that way) failure. It also means facing the blank page and starting all over again.

Whether we like it or not, sooner or later we perfectionists have to stop using revision as a means of avoiding the inevitable. *The perfect is the enemy of the good.* We have to let go.

1 In fact it was Sir Arthur Quiller-Couch in *The Art of Writing* (1916): "Whenever you feel an impulse to perpetrate a piece of exceptionally fine writing, obey it—whole-heartedly—and delete it before sending your manuscript to press. Murder your darlings."

But *when* should we let go? The answer came to me in a dream. Struggle long and hard and you too will have a dream in which you tear open a letter of acceptance from a publisher. My dream had this twist: the letter was in a box with my manuscript. Now normally, when manuscripts are returned, it means one thing—rejection. But when I opened the box I saw a strange thing: the words "GREAT ENOUGH" stamped in red ink across the title page. Then I read the letter in which the editor explained that, flawed though my novel certainly was, he had found it of sufficient merit to slap between covers. It was "great enough."

And that, folks, is when we ought to relinquish our works: not when they are good, or good enough, or great, but when they are great enough. When they are great enough the law of diminishing returns will have set in: Whatever changes you make from then on won't be worth the effort, or worse, will undermine what you've achieved.

Some authors claim they never really finish their works —they abandon them. Then there are those who know when the work is done; when all the planets have aligned themselves, when form and meaning are so of a piece they are indistinguishable, and every word feels inevitable, if not carved in stone. For me, it's like raising children. At a certain age, ready or not, out they go. They must complete themselves in the cruel, cold world. Perhaps some of our stories will never please certain people; maybe they'll never be universally loved and admired. There's nothing to be done; it's out of our hands. You must think of your other children, including those yet to be born.

A few final words on revision: One writer I know once

described what he does most of every day as laying mortar between bricks. The bricks are bursts of inspiration: They come to us as scenes, characters, lines of dialogue, plot twists, whole paragraphs. The mortar is the stuff that holds those inspirations together.

Rarely are our stories made of either pure bricks or pure mortar: They usually hold a few bricks of inspiration between blobs of gray cement. It's the mortar that takes all of the effort: first, to try and use as little as possible; and second, to make it blend seamlessly with the bricks.

It comes down to this: Writing is work. There's no automatic pilot for the controls, no painting by numbers. If that's not enough bad news, writing also takes talent. The good news is that great fiction doesn't require Shakespeare's poetry or Joyce's genius. Cunning and craft will do. And though they may not achieve it, your stories and novels can approach art.

That's the purpose of revision, to approach art.

CHAPTER X:
Inspiration, Perspiration, Publication

*"Posterity—what you write for after being
turned down by publishers."*
—George Ade

X. INSPIRATION, PERSPIRATION, PUBLICATION

Though most of us write something in our lives, if only laundry lists or love letters, writing as a serious vocation isn't for everyone. Even if you take your writing very seriously, that doesn't mean you have to publish, or to want to publish. In her lifetime Emily Dickinson published none of her poetry. Others, like Harper Lee *(To Kill a Mockingbird)* and Ralph Ellison *(Invisible Man)* published one tremendous novel each, then all but disappeared. Thomas Hardy, embittered by rotten reviews of his fiction, turned his back on the novel, producing only poetry for the rest of his years. J.D. Salinger was still a young man with a brilliant career behind (and presumably ahead) of him when he ducked into the New Hampshire woods, never to be seen in print again

For every artist who dares to hawk his wears in public, there must be ten dozen more who hide their light under a bushel, never exposing it to the winds of criticism. Rejection hurts. Once sent out into the world, our creations are defenseless against critics who, according to Kurt Vonnegut, "put on full armor [to attack] a banana split." We build fictional worlds out of the delicate stuff of dreams. And the world swings its mace.

"Fiction completes us," wrote Mario Vargas Llosa, "mutilated beings burdened with the awful dichotomy of having only one life and the ability to desire a thousand." Those of us willing to take our products to market accept this burden not just for ourselves, but on behalf of all those who would rather read than write.

But if we're to take on that burden, we must be prepared to face down rejection and despair. Except for a lucky few, the fortune of publication doesn't come without slings and arrows.

2. PERSISTENCE

I once attended a "Life After Graduate School" panel discussion by a group of recent graduates of a prestigious MFA creative writing program. The panelists held forth on, among other topics, the tribulations they and fellow classmates had endured in the two years since graduating. Though several had gone on to win publishing contracts, most had seen the rejection letter on the wall and called it quits, turning instead to safer, more lucrative careers in advertising, medicine, law, and dog walking.

"They gave up," one of the panelists said.

"You call that giving up?" I said. "I call it never starting!"

Having written for over a quarter of a century with several thousand rejection slips to show for it, I felt entitled to this self-righteous outburst. But the fact is that anyone who quits writing after two, three, ten, or even twenty years probably never had it in her or him to be a real writer in the first place, since *real writers never give up.* They can't; they have no choice. For them writing isn't a career choice or even a lifestyle, but a way of living. They can no more give up writing than a fish can give up swimming or a woodpecker can give up pecking wood. Simply, it's what they do.

Occasionally students come to me and say something like, "I'm giving this writing business five years. If by then I haven't published a book, then it's back to daddy's ball-bearing factory." To this grave threat my response is always along these lines: "By all means work in dad's ball-busting—um—ball-bearing factory, if it suits you. As to whether or not you keep writing, the choice isn't yours to make."

I have a similar set response to students who complain to me about my own or someone else's criticism of their work. "Thanks to so-and-so, I'll never put pen to paper again," they declare. To which solemn oath I reply, "You may never put pen to paper, but it won't be thanks to anyone but yourself."

Then there are the earnest ones who ask, "Do you think I have any talent? Am I *good enough?* Am I *really* a writer?" I have to remind them that a writer is someone who writes, and keeps writing, no matter what. And while there is such a thing as talent, and while it isn't equally or equitably distributed, talent isn't usually enough. What counts more is perseverance.

So, to answer their questions, "If you persist, then you're really a writer."

No one can stop a real writer from writing. On the other hand if for you writing is merely a means of winning praise and acceptance, you'll either write fatuous, derivative, crowd-pleasing drivel, or enter a world of hurt.

I say write only for yourself, for your highest and humblest self, for the integral you whose world view is as solid as Gibraltar, and whose faith and idealism—when it comes to art, anyway—know no bounds.

And never say die.

3. PERSPIRATION: GETTING THE WORK OUT

As I've remarked, publishing is a business. And not a gentleman's trade, as once, but a corporate military campaign whose war cry is 8 percent growth per annum: a Darwinian contest sponsored by Death Star conglomerates and marketing consultants who—whatever they may say to the contrary—don't give a fig about good writing.

We don't write for marketing execs any more than we write for our mothers or our teachers. But we do write for an audience, and in consideration of them we do our very best. That audience may be wide or slim, but it is made of those people whose opinions matter to us almost as much as as our own. They—not the critics, not the marketing people, not our parents—are the only judges who count.

Those of us who've had the privilege to work with good agents and editors understand that they serve as proxies for our audience: They guide us in making decisions about what to write, how to write it, whether a book or story is ready for "out there." And if not, why not.

But getting an editor or an agent is close to the last of many hurdles. The first is getting published. That seems paradoxical. But before entering the major leagues, you'll want to rack up some minor-league credits. That means submitting to and publishing in what are called "little" magazines.

4. The "Little" Magazines

Probably the first things you'll publish will be stories. You'll send them out yourself to some of the many fine journals and reviews out there. The *little* in *little magazines* refers to the fact that these magazines tend to be physically small in size and to have low circulation numbers—between 500 and 5,000. By no means should *little* be taken for a negative judgment, since by and large these magazines are of extremely high quality both in design and in the caliber of the work they publish. And they're extremely competitive.

Most literary reviews are supported by universities or colleges, or run by private publishers, and are devoted exclusively to creative writing, to poetry, fiction, and essays, and in some cases to critical writing and reviews. They may also be your best, if not your only, bet. *Harpers,* the *New Yorker, Playboy*, *Esquire* or *GQ* also print fiction, but the odds of being published in one of these hallowed venues are no better than those of being struck by lightning.

Not that you shouldn't try to publish in the *New Yorker*. After all, should you succeed, you'd not only be paid handsomely (five dollars a word at last check), but more than likely you'd be approached by several drooling agents. However, though the *New Yorker* claims to read all its unsolicited (i.e., unagented) submissions, I've never known anyone to get an "over the transom" piece accepted there, ever. (The phrase *over-the-transom* refers to the days when unsolicited parcels were literally flung through the open transoms of editor's doors).[1] To be seriously considered by the *New Yorker*, you need to have an agent submit for you. And most agents are loath to submit short stories except for their established—and already profitable—clients.

So start with the little magazines. Which little magazines to submit to? Decide for yourself. Go to the nearest surviving mega bookstore chain. At many Barnes & Noble you'll find dozens of literary reviews gathered in the magazine stacks. I tell my students what I'll tell you: to go there, grab a pile, sit down in the café, and—while taking care not to spill coffee or pastry crumbs on the pages—read as many as you can, seeing which stories have something in common with yours, thematically or in level of accomplishment. Write down any submission guidelines, if provided. Jot down each magazine's Web address and look them up later online (easier than ever to do now through search engine websites like Duotope: https://duotrope.com/).

Make a list of at least two dozen little magazines. From among them choose one to subscribe to, and do so. It'll put something nice in your mailbox. And it's good karma.

While in the magazine section, look for the latest *Poets & Writers*, a publication indispensable to serious writers. In it you'll find interesting reviews and articles about books and authors, as well as information on conferences and retreats, MFA programs, awards and fellowships, and literary magazines seeking submissions. You should probably subscribe to it, too. Each month when a new issue comes, I take an hour to read through it, circling (in red pen) contest

1 Don't try this.

deadlines and other items of interest.

While still in the bookstore, ask for the section of books on writing. There you'll find reference books like the *Novel and Short Story Writer's Market*, published annually. In such books you'll find not only catalogues of literary magazines, but also lists of agents and publishers accepting fiction, interviews with up-and-coming authors, and articles with titles like "Write that Killer Query Letter" (which you needn't read, since I'm about to to tell you how to do so). Make sure with such books that you get the latest edition, since magazines and their editors change with the seasons.

Armed with these resources you should be able to compile a solid list of twenty-five to thirty places to send your stories to. These should range from easier-to-break-into fledglings to the legendarily insurmountable *Paris Review*. Select ten or more and submit your best, polished-to-a-fare-thee-well story to all.

Should any of these journals have rules against simultaneous submissions, damn them. Don't announce that you're damning them; just do it. Worst-case scenario, you'll have your story accepted by two magazines and will have to confess your crime to an editor who won't be pleased, and may even foam slightly at the mouth. Should this unlikely scenario arise, offer the foaming editor an exclusive on your next best story.

This may appease him, or not. But in this age where publications take six to eight months to respond to submissions, you can't afford to send your stories to one place at a time. Frankly it's unfair and unreasonable of editors to make this request in exchange for which nothing of equal value is offered.

5. THE MECHANICS OF SUBMISSION

If you wish, say, to submit a story inspired by life on your widowed mother's ranch, you would write a simple cover letter to Editor or Fiction Editor saying that you have enclosed "Mother's Milk," a story of 8,000 words, for his consideration. Then add a paragraph about your writing credentials (if any), or anything in your background pertaining to the submitted work ("I grew up on my mother's dairy farm, which had a hundred head of cattle and which she ran single-handedly after my father was struck by a freight train")—something to pique a jaded editor's interest.

Not that cover letters matter all that much, since in the end the story alone will count. I edit a literary review and read for several others, and if I read cover letters at all I do so after reading the submission, if only for the shock of discovering that an author whose story seemed to me amateurish has published in the *New Yorker*, or that an author whose work I adore has never been published anywhere. Either way I'm not influenced. The story is still the story.

Put a copy of your submission, paper-clipped, with your name and contact information on the first (title) page, in an envelope with the cover letter and an SASE—a self-addressed, stamped envelope. (Send an SASE large enough to hold your manuscript if you want it returned; send a no. 10 business envelope if you don't. A self-adhesive flap will spare your arbiters the bitterness of envelope glue.) Once your package is assembled, apply postage and send it off.

Many literary magazines now accept online submissions, so you may want to check the submission guidelines before printing out your story. With online submissions, you fill in a database and, in the comments box, add a short note including your biographical information. Then upload your story as a pdf or word.doc and submit.

However and wherever you send your work, be sure you send it during the period when the publications are open to submissions. Most places don't read during the summer months, but there are exceptions

Important: Keep good records of where you've sent what.

Then forget about it. Within weeks you'll start getting e-mails with the subject heading "Your Submission to ——," or finding envelopes addressed to you in your own handwriting in your mailbox: your prodigal children returning home. One of those emails or envelopes might hold good news. Probably not. For every story the little magazines accept, they reject dozens.

When you do get a rejection slip—and you will—don't feel bad. Think of it as part of the process, with each rejection slip a rung on the ladder mounting toward acceptance. The more rejections you get, the closer you are to publishing heaven. Be proud of each rejection: You worked hard for it. *Do not despair and never say die.*

When good news does come it will most often come in the form of an e-mail or a telephone call from an editor saying she wants to publish your story. She may have some editorial suggestions or demands. If so, take them, or at least take them seriously. Most editors working for literary reviews do what they do out of love and devotion. And they know their stuff. If they ask for changes, it's probably for a good reason. And anyway it shows that they've read your work closely.

Then again, sometimes you need to stick to your guns. An editor once had me truncate the ending of a story. I did, but regretted it. Usually, if you can put up a solid defense of your choices, editors will listen, and ultimately defer to you, the writer, and so they should.

When a story keeps getting rejected—say, more than a dozen times—consider revising it before sending it out again. Some of my best stories were rejected for years before finding homes in excellent reviews. Meanwhile I improved them. To be well-published was worth the time and effort.

A short list of popular "little magazines":

The Paris Review
Tin House
A Public Space
Zoetrope All-Story
Ploughshares
Virginia Quarterly Review
Glimmer Train
Boulevard
Granta
Missouri Review
Witness
Gettysburg Review
Kenyon Review

Massachusetts Review
Prairie Schooner
Mid-America Review
New England Review
Story Quarterly
The Literary Review
One-story
Bellingham Review
North Dakota Quarterly
New Millennium
Gulf Coast
Florida Review
Arts & Letters

This is by no means an exhaustive list. There are hundreds of fine reviews out there, and new ones coming out all the time. Check the back pages of *Poets & Writers* for the latest new litmags seeking submissions.

6. WHAT EDITORS DO AND DON'T WANT

The difference between persistence and wasting your time may boil down to understanding that editors are people with a job to do, and that job consists of finding material to fill the pages of their publications. For every page they have to fill, they get somewhere between a hundred and ten thousand pages of material. They can afford to be fussy, and you can't blame them for being jaded.

They'll tell you that they want good writing, which of course is true. But good writing alone won't cut it. They want to see something they and the readers of their magazines haven't seen a thousand times before, a fresh style, subject, voice, or point of view.

To try and second-guess what, exactly, will turn editors on is impossible. Even if you could guess, I don't suggest that you try. Again, you have to write what you want to write, which (hopefully) corresponds to what you and others want to read.

That said, there are some stories few editors are interested in and that should probably be kept safe in file drawers:

1. **The and-then-she-woke-up story,** in which the outcome of the plot is entirely contingent upon capriciously withheld information.

2. **The what-I-did-on-my-summer-vacation story,** in which unadulterated autobiographical anecdotes are recycled.

3. **The I-don't-get-out-much story,** in which the present action consists almost exclusively of a character getting out of bed and/or brushing his or her teeth.

4. **The implausible-if-not-altogether-impossible story,** in which an incredible amount happens incredibly.

5. **The "Vas you der, Charley?" story,** in which everything of interest takes place off-stage and to characters other than the protagonist.

6. **The Albert Camus commemorative story,** in which characters who want nothing in particular wander gritty city streets in an existential haze.

7. **The Sylvia Plath commemorative story,** in which the protagonist has just been released from or is bound for a mental institution.

8. **The postmodern MacGuffin story,** in which the protagonist mounts an obsessive quest for the perfect jalapeño pepper or some such trivial object.

9. **The woe-is-my-hero/heroine story,** in which the protagonist is a victim of everyone and everything.

10. **The next-time-try-a-church story,** in which characters of opposite sexes, one of whom turns out to be a psychopath, meet in a bar, elevator, supermarket check-out aisle, or AA meeting.

11. **The unbridled-time-machine story,** in which the narrative flashes so often and abruptly backwards and forwards in time the reader gets whiplash.

12. **The have-I-got-your-attention-now? story,** in which a character is dismembered in the opening paragraph.

13. **The "Who asked?" story,** in whch an outcome is posited to a ludicrously hypothetical situation (e.g., what if Mick

Jagger and Margaret Thatcher were the only two survivors of a nuclear holocaust?).

14. **The excuse-me-but-did-you-know? … story,** in which an erudite narrator, with no discernable plot in sight, regales the reader with lore on one or more of the following: submarines, dinosaurs, viruses, the Civil War, insects, anthropology, or curry powder.

15. **The analyze-this story,** in which characters perform grotesque and gratuitous acts designed to call into question their author's mental health (see #'s 7, 19).

16. **The I'm-enlightened-he/she-isn't story,** in which the hero or heroine rekindles a past love affair, only to discover that he/she has outgrown it.

17. **The suck-on-this-you-bitch/bastard story,** in which the hero or heroine avenges him/herself of the evil doings of an parent, spouse, or ex-lover.

18. **The I-forgive-you-you-bitch/bastard story,** in which the hero/heroine visits a dying evil parent, spouse, or ex-lover in nursing home or hospital.

19. **The I-really-don't-know-why-I'm-telling-you-this story,** in which the narrator is hell-bent on degrading himself with insights into, for example, his flatulence.

There are, to be sure, other kinds of less-than-sought-after stories, but they tend to be variants of the types listed above. I'm just letting you know that, if you've written one of these, you're not the first to bark up that particular tree.

Mind you, the truly fearless among you will roll up your sleeves, damn the torpedoes, and produce a variation of one of the above plots so dazzling an editor will not only publish it, he'll grovel at your feet and nominate you for a MacArthur genius award.

7. AGENTS

To nab an agent you typically need a book-length work—a novel or a collection of stories of between 150 and 400 pages. These days books of stories are a hard sell, hence less attractive to agents (unless you've published one of them in a top-tier review or in the *New Yorker*—unlikely without an agent: catch-22).

Assuming you've got such a work ready or close to ready, you need to research those agents who are open to queries, come up with a list, and query them. As with the little magazines, through research you'll narrow the list down to, say, forty or so (there are hundreds of agents, too). If the book you've written bears comparison with something out there, find out who the book's agent was. Check the acknowledgements page. Or call the publisher and ask for the publicity or editorial department. They'll tell you.

Next, write that killer query letter. It should consist of a personalized opening ("We met at the Sewanee Writer's Conference" or "I'm a big fan of John C. Beezelbub's novel, *Wine Without the Glass,* which I understand you represent") followed by a description of the book you've written, followed by a short biography, and then a closing line explaining that the work is available for consideration.

But why tell you how to write a query letter when I can show you?

The following—or something very much like it—was written by a student with a little help from me, her instructor. My student's agent having forbidden me from quoting the original (which he called a "private correspondence," despite an idential missive having been dispatched to forty-seven of his brethren), I have changed names and altered language, but the gist remains the same:

Dear Ms. Agent,

"Your problem, Ms. Davenport, is that you don't seem to know the difference between what people believe and what's true."

"Sure I do, Clyde. The difference is there is no difference. That's what makes me a good reporter. Folks believe me. And we live in an age of belief, or haven't you noticed?"

Meet Mandy Davenport: a plucky gal from Comersville, Mississippi, who tears herself up from her swampy Delta roots to seek her fortune as a journalist in New York City. When her southern charms and impressive CV land her a job with the ultra right-wing Hyena News Network, she's plunged into a world of ruthless misogynists willing to do anything to advance their political ideologies and their careers. While spinning propaganda for Hyena, Mandy dates Clyde Wentworth, an old flame from down south, now a Pulitzer-winning reporter for a struggling liberal newspaper. She's also courted by Bernard T. Rex, Chairman and CEO of Hyena Media Enterprises, one of the most powerful and ruthless men in the world and old enough to be her grandfather.

Can Mandy become the youngest news anchor in America without shedding her dignity and her morals? Or will she risk everything—including possibly her life—to expose the world's most influential, and corrupt, news organization?

A veteran morning anchor with Wolf News Channel and several other network news stations, I have ten years' experience as an insider in the fast-paced, high-anxiety, sex, drug, scandal-and-treachery-ridden world of ultra-conservative broadcast news. My background, combined with a rather overripe imagination, has inspired me to write *A Hyena in Sheep's Clothing,* Mandy's story.

The opening chapters of my nearly completed manuscript are available upon request.

Thank you, Ms. Agent, for your time and consideration. I look forward to hearing back from you in the near future.

Warmest Regards,
Ashley Penbroke

As indicated, I've had to modify "Ashley's" letter to protect her and her agent's privacy. And though the result may sound like a spoof, it's quite close to the original—which, by the way, garnered seventeen (seventeen!) positive responses, from among the forty-seven agents queried, including some from the most powerful agents in town. Ultimately, "Ashley's" novel sold to a reputable house for a sum veering on six figures—this despite that scarcely a word of it had been written. Such "pig in the poke" sales are indeed rare for first novels. But then this writer's timing couldn't have been better: a chick-lit novel featuring an insider's glimpse into right-wing media. Only one question remained: Could they get it on the shelves by Election Day?

This brings me to an issue that cannot be brushed aside. As a callow young literary agent was shameless enough to actually admit to me, "These days it's not location anymore —it's *platform, platform, platform.*" By which he meant that more and more books are being sold not based on the quality of their contents, but on the biographies (read: marketability) of their authors. Young? Attractive? Exotic? Harvard or Yale Graduate? Great: now all we need is a novel; a trivial matter. I wanted to remind this agent that, platform to whatever power notwithstanding, in the end good writing still counts, and counts more than all the rest—that is, assuming that eventually people will actually *read* what publishers publish and bookstores sell. But I knew better than to waste my breath on this fellow who, like too many agents and editors these days, holds artistic values hostage to commercial ones. Sure, he'll sell books. But he may as well trade frozen pork rinds on the futures market.

Enough of my rant. We're talking about *your* book, which has been an *artistic* undertaking. Still, you must sell it. And to do so you'll need a snappy query letter that wastes no time and puts no premium on subtlety or modesty, or, for that matter, good taste. While conveying what you've written accurately, it must also grab an agent's attention.

When an agent says yes, unless you specify otherwise you owe him an exclusive look at your book, which may take six weeks or so. After the agreed-upon time period you may want to send a follow-up e-mail requesting a progress report. Since your work is now being tied up, you're entitled to put some pressure on. But go easy: Too much pressure and he'll think twice about having you as a client.

Hopefully, the happy day will come when an agent will take you on. Hopefully, he'll be the right agent for you and your work. With luck, he'll sell your book—or at least he'll try his damndest to sell it. Note that good agents always provide their clients with letters of rejection from editors to whom they've shown the work. If they don't, you should ask. And if the letters are not forthcoming, consider seeking a more professional agent.

8. PUBLICATION

> *"Success is a rare paint; hides all the ugliness."*
> —Sir John Suckling

Once your agent sells the book, you'll be put in touch with the purchasing editor, who will probably request changes to your manuscript (some agents will also give you editorial advice; welcome it). You and your editor will work closely to see to it that the book that gets printed is the very best book possible. You may have disagreements, in which case all things being equal defer to your editor, since he has been at this sort of thing longer than you.

The advance for a first novel by a commercial publisher can be anything from a couple thousand dollars to hundreds of thousands, ten to twenty thousand being typical, depending on the size of the publisher and on the quality of the book, and whether it has *bestseller* written all over it or not.

Smaller publishers pay less—or nothing at all—up front. And then there are those publishers who ask authors to contribute to the cost of designing, promoting, and publishing their work. Whatever they may call themselves, these are subsidy publishers. And while strictly speaking there's nothing wrong with contributing to the cost of publishing your own work, it does call into question the publisher's standards and motives. Put another way, a publisher's sincere and serious commitment to your work exists usually in direct proportion to his willingness to *lose* money on you.

This is why I don't think much of "publishing" through IUniverse. Yes, it gets you around agents and editors and publishers and all of those potentially dreadful people. On the other hand it gets you around wonderful agents and editor and publishers, people who could do you and your book enormous good—possibly even by not publishing it when it's not ready or fit to be published. The so-called "guardians at the gate" aren't always malevolent, or purely so. And even if your book is worthy, how will you know it if you publish it yourself? Because your friends say so? Why not just give the book to your mother and have her praise it? Compliments from friends mean nothing. Compliments from strangers mean slightly more. But when professionals judge your work and deem it publishable—*that* means something.

Whatever the woes of the publishing world, there are still enough small publishers with integrity out there so that, until you've exhausted them all, you have no excuse for throwing your hands in the air and surrendering to IUniverse or its equivalent. And anyway a publisher who's willing to publish anything is no better than the Internet: i.e., a reservoir that anyone can drink from, and anyone can pee into.[2]

2 I first wrote these words in 2005. Since then the boom in self-publishing has given me cause to rethink them, which I have, but my feelings remain the same. Publishing your own book is like kissing a mirror. It

Then again it would be a mistake to tie our work's value to any financial judgment. Gorgeous writing—even in service of exquisite stories—doesn't always translate into dollars and cents, nor does it always or even often spell bestseller. In terms of prose style, most bestsellers aren't well-written (for a flagrant example see *The DaVinci Code*, or any number of so-called "airport" books*)*. Not that they're necessarily bad, they're just not usually that good.

Which begs the question: Why, all things (plot, characters, etc.) being equal, do badly written books outsell beautifully written ones? For the same reason, I guess, that McDonald's is presently the world's most popular eating establishment. And Cheese Doodles sell better than real cheese.

9. INSPIRATION

I weary of publishing talk. Much of the reality sounds so dreadful. And yet we hear stories, too, of great sudden success, wealth, and fairytale fame (J.K. Rowling). We cling to those stories—well, some of us do. To those who find solace in such tales, I say good for them. No point explaining to them that we remember such stories because they're the exception, not the rule.

For most of us the tale will be much more prosaic, with years of hard work and rejection punctuated, like the night sky with stars, by small moments of triumph. But then the work keeps getting better, and the work is all that matters.

may be expedient, but it's nothing like the real thing. Then again there are so many fine small publishers out there, more than ever. At the very least try some of them first.

Chapter X

Repeat: *the work is all that matters, the work is all that matters. ...*

"... Do you know what you will be asked when you die? But first let me tell you what you won't be asked. You won't be asked if you were working on a wonderful, moving piece of writing when you died. You won't be asked if it was long or short, sad or funny, published or unpublished. You won't be asked if you were in good or bad form while you were working on it. You won't even be asked if it was the one piece of writing you would have been working on if you had known your time would be up when it was finished. ... I'm sure you'll be asked only two questions. Were most of your stars out? Were you busy writing your heart out? If only you knew how easy it would be for you to say yes to both of those questions. If only you'd remember before you ever sit down to write that you've been a reader long before you were ever a writer. You simply fix that fact in your mind, then sit very still and ask yourself, as a reader, what piece of writing in all the world Buddy Glass would most want to read if he had his heart's choice. The next step is terrible, but so simple I can hardly believe it as I write it. You just sit down shamelessly and write the thing yourself."

— J. D. Salinger, *Seymour: an Introduction*

The work is all that matters ...
Now sit down and get to work.

SELECTED BIBLIOGRAPHY

BOOKS ON CRAFT:

Aristotle. *Poetics*. New York: Hill and Wang, 1963.

Braine, John. *Writing a Novel*. New York: McGraw-Hill, 1975.

Cary, Joyce. *Art and Reality*. New York: Harper, 1958.

Forster, E.M. *Aspects of the Novel*. New York: Harcourt, Brace, 1956.

Gardner, John. *The Art of Fiction*. New York: Vintage Books, 1985.

Gornick, Vivian. *The Situation and the Story: The Art of Personal Narrative*. New York: Farrar, Straus & Giroux, 2002.

Lamott, Anne. *Bird by Bird*. New York: Anchor Books, 1995.

Lodge, David. *The Art of Fiction*. New York: Viking, 1993.

Madden, David. *Revising Fiction*. New York: New American Library, 1988.

McCullers, Carson. *Illumination and Night Glare: The Unfinished Autobiography of Carson McCullers*. Madison: University of Wisconsin Press, 1999.

Newlove, Donald. *First Paragraphs*. New York: St. Martin's Press, 1992.

O'Connor, Flannery. *Mystery and Manners: Occasional Prose*. New York: Farrar, Straus, & Giroux, 1969.

Plimpton, George, ed. *The Writer's Chapbook*. New York: Viking, 1989.

Strunk, William Jr. and E.B. White. *The Elements of Style*. New York: Macmillan, 1972.

Surmelian, Leon. *Techniques of Fiction Writing; Measure and Madness*. Garden City, N.Y.: Doubleday, 1968.

Woolf, Virginia. *A Writer's Diary*. New York: Harcourt, Brace, 1954.

PETER SELGIN is the author of *Drowning Lessons*, winner of the 2007 Flannery O'Connor Award for Fiction, *Life Goes to the Movies*, a novel, and several children's books. His memoir, *Confessions of a Left-Handed Man: An Artist's Memoir*, was short-listed for the 2012 William Saroyan International Prize for Writing. His most recent novel, *The Water Master*, was awarded the Pirate's Alley William Faulkner Society Prize for Best Novel. Other honors include the Missouri Review Editors' Prize, the Dana Award for the Essay, and a Eugene O'Neill National Playwrights' Conference Fellowship for his full-length play, *A God in the House*, based on Dr. Kevorkian and his suicide machine. He is Assistant Professor of Creative Writing at Georgia College & State University and teaches at Antioch University's Graduate MFA Writing Program.

CPSIA information can be obtained
at www.ICGtesting.com
Printed in the USA
LVHW042313170621
690500LV00011B/1275

9 780985 849535